Enjoy wholesome hearty dinners
even on your busiest days!

DOESN'T it seem like life just keeps getting busier? Work, school, errands…the list goes on and on. Squeezing in time for eating meals is difficult, let alone the time to cook them. Drive-thru and take-out seem like good choices because they're speedy, but in the long run, they're not satisfying.

This book will take a big load off your shoulders because it puts an end to the "What's for Dinner?" dilemma—with wholesome, home-cooked dinners in a snap.

Taste of Home's Weeknight Cooking Made Easy 2005 is packed with 202 mouth-watering recipes that let you get a tasty, homemade dinner on the table in mere minutes. Here's what sets this one-of-a-kind cookbook apart from all others:

● **Fresh ingredients.** *Taste of Home's Weeknight Cooking Made Easy 2005* doesn't rely heavily on packaged, processed foods to get dinner done fast. Rather, we provide a balance of fresh and convenience foods to provide more from-scratch goodness.

● **Focus on main dishes.** Entrees are the meat and potatoes to meal planning. You'll find 154 main dishes, featuring beef, ground beef, chicken, turkey, pork and seafood in addition to meatless entree ideas.

● **Speed is key.** This book offers 165 recipes that go from start to finish in less than 30 minutes. (And 39 of those recipes can be ready in under 15 minutes!)

● **Beautiful photos.** We know you're more likely to try recipes with a picture. So we've included a gorgeous, color photo of *each and every* recipe!

● **Prep and cooking times.** The preparation and cooking times for each dish are prominently displayed, making it easy to find recipes that fit your schedule.

● **More than 300 helpful hints.** Each recipe features at least one timely tip, such as tricks that reduce preparation time, facts for buying and storing foods, substitution secrets and ideas for speedy side dishes.

● **Easy on the eyes.** *Taste of Home's Weeknight Cooking Made Easy 2005* is so easy to read because there is only one recipe on a page.

● **Recipe list by chapter.** Quickly browse through the recipes in each chapter without turning a page! Just go to the beginning of each chapter for the list of recipes.

With *Taste of Home's Weeknight Cooking Made Easy 2005*, offering your family a wholesome meal night after night couldn't be easier!

Weeknight Cooking Made Easy 2005

Taste of Home Books
©2005 Reiman Media Group, Inc.
5400 S. 60th St., Greendale WI 53129
International Standard Book Number: 0-89821-446-7
International Standard Serial Number: 1555-0400

For additional copies of this book, write *Taste of Home*
Books, P.O. Box 908, Greendale WI 53129. Or to order
by credit card, call toll-free 1-800/344-2560 or visit
our Web site at **www.reimanpub.com**.

PICTURED ON THE COVER:
Vegetable Beef Ragout (p. 45)

Senior Editor: Julie Schnittka

Senior Art Director: Linda Dzik

Executive Editor, Books:
Heidi Reuter Lloyd

Associate Editor: Jean Steiner

Graphic Art Associates:
Ellen Lloyd, Catherine Fletcher

Editorial Assistant: Barb Czysz

Food Editor:
Janaan Cunningham

Associate Food Editor:
Diane Werner RD

Senior Recipe Editor:
Sue A. Jurack

Test Kitchen Director:
Mark Morgan RD

Recipe Developer:
Dot Vartan

Test Kitchen Assistant:
Kris Lehman

Food Photographers:
Rob Hagen, Dan Roberts

Set Stylists: Julie Ferron,
Stephanie Marchese, Sue Myers,
Jennifer Bradley Vent

Food Stylists: Kristin Arnett,
Sarah Thompson, Joylyn Trickel

Photographers Assistant:
Lori Foy

**Senior Vice President, Editor
in Chief:** Catherine Cassidy

President: Barbara Newton

Chairman and Founder:
Roy Reiman

Easy Weekday Menus

Whether you're eating on the run or actually able to enjoy a relaxing sit-down dinner, the following pages offer innovative ways to turn recipes from *Weeknight Cooking Made Easy* into complete meals in minutes!

After-Soccer Supper

Serves 6

As soon as you get home from work, you and the kids are heading out the door for soccer practice. Take comfort in knowing a delightful slow-cooker dinner will be waiting when you get home!

Slow-Cooked Swiss Steak (p. 67)
Blue Cheese Mashed Potatoes (p. 266)
Frozen broccoli florets
Assorted purchased cookies

Cooking for Two

Serves 2

When the kids are away for the evening, why not indulge in a wonderful meal for just the two of you?

Salmon Patties with
Caper Mayonnaise (p. 229)
Mixed Greens with Goat Cheese
(p. 256)
Bakery brownies

Special Celebration

Serves 4

Special occasions don't always wait for the weekend. Celebrate a job promotion, stellar report card or sporting achievement with this easy yet elegant menu.

Basil Cream Chicken (p. 115)
Rice pilaf
Mousse in Waffle Bowls (p. 298)

A Taste of the Tropics

Serves 4

Give your family a vacation from cool winter winds with this heart-warming menu reminiscent of a tropical location.

Ham with Mango Salsa (p. 169)
Fresh bread or rolls
Warm Banana Crepes (p. 313)

Grill-Side Goodies

Serves 4

Escape the heat of the kitchen by cooking the entree and sides on the grill. End the meal with a cool dessert. It's a great way to relax on a summer night.

Zesty Grilled Chops (p. 171)
Grilled Asparagus (p. 259)
Grilled corn on the cob
Cheery Cherry Parfaits (p. 304)

Italian Cuisine

Serves 4

There's no need to venture out to an Italian restaurant when you can create a taste of Little Italy right at home!

Gnocchi with Pesto Sauce (p. 193)
Crisp Side Salad (p. 284)
Tasty Tiramisu (p. 292)

Down-Home Dinner

Serves 8

Comfort foods aren't restricted to Sunday dinner with this trio of time-saving recipes.

Turkey Meat Loaf (p. 143)
Sweet Potatoes 'n' Pears (p. 277)
Apple Gingerbread Cake (p. 300)

Orient Express

Serves 4

You don't need to pick up takeout when you have a hankering for Asian cooking!

Gingered Pepper Steak (p. 46)
Thai Vegetable Noodles (p. 205)
Egg rolls
Fortune cookies

Friday Night Football Fare

Serves 8

Before heading out to watch the big game, tackle the appetites of your family and a few friends by serving satisfying sandwiches.

Teriyaki Pulled Pork Sandwiches
(p. 187)
Roasted Veggie Pasta Salad (p. 206)
Potato or corn chips
Hazelnut Cheesecake Dessert (p. 311)

Make It Mexican!

Serves 4

When your family craves south-of-the-border cuisine, rely on this speedy supper.

Santa Fe Enchiladas (p. 32)
Spanish rice
Corn with a Kick (p. 278)
Cinnamon or chocolate ice cream

From burgers and stews to casseroles and stir-frys, ground beef stars in a splendid assortment of enticing entrees.

Hominy Beef Polenta
(p. 20)

Speedy Ground Beef

Sweet-and-Sour Meatballs

PREP/TOTAL TIME: 30 min.

   1 can (20 ounces) pineapple chunks
 1/2 cup packed brown sugar
   3 tablespoons cornstarch
 1/3 cup cold water
   3 tablespoons cider vinegar
   1 tablespoon soy sauce
  30 frozen fully cooked meatballs, thawed (1/2 ounce each) (15 ounces)
   1 large green pepper, cut into 1-inch pieces
Hot cooked rice, optional

Drain pineapple, reserving juice. Set pineapple aside. Add water to juice if needed to measure 1 cup; pour into a large skillet. In a bowl, combine the brown sugar, cornstarch, cold water, vinegar and soy sauce until smooth. Stir into skillet.

Bring to a boil over medium heat; cook and stir until thickened. Add pineapple, meatballs and green pepper. Simmer, uncovered, for 20 minutes or until heated through. Serve with rice if desired.

Yield: 6 servings.

Nutritional Analysis: 5 meatballs with about 1/2 cup sauce (calculated without rice) equals 226 calories, 5 g fat (2 g saturated fat), 29 mg cholesterol, 206 mg sodium, 40 g carbohydrate, 1 g fiber, 7 g protein.

More Meaty Meals

Frozen fully cooked meatballs are a great meal starter to keep in the freezer. Thaw them and add to your favorite spaghetti sauce. Then serve over pasta or on sandwich rolls.

Thickening with Cornstarch

Cornstarch clumps easily. So before stirring it into a hot mixture, add a small amount of cold liquid to the cornstarch to form a thin paste.

Stir constantly as you add the cornstarch paste to a hot liquid, bringing the mixture to a boil. Cook for about 2 minutes, stirring often, for the mixture to obtain maximum thickness.

Cuban-Style Stuffed Peppers

PREP/TOTAL TIME: 25 min.

1 pound lean ground beef
1/2 cup chopped onion
2 teaspoons minced garlic
2 teaspoons olive oil
1 can (14-1/2 ounces) diced tomatoes
  with mild green chilies
1 cup cooked long grain rice
1/4 cup dry red wine
1/4 cup sliced stuffed olives
3 tablespoons tomato paste
2 teaspoons dried oregano
1 teaspoon salt
1/2 teaspoon pepper
4 large green peppers
1 cup water
Roasted sweet red pepper strips, optional

In a large skillet, cook beef, onion and garlic in oil over medium heat until meat is no longer pink; drain. Stir in the next eight ingredients. Bring to a boil. Reduce heat; simmer, uncovered, for 15-20 minutes.

Meanwhile, cut green peppers in half lengthwise; discard seeds. Place in an ungreased shallow 3-qt. microwave-safe dish; add water. Cover and microwave on high for 8-10 minutes or until crisp-tender. Drain; fill each pepper half with 1/2 cup meat mixture. Garnish with red pepper strips if desired.

Editor's Note: This recipe was tested in a 1,100-watt microwave.

Yield: 4 servings.

Nutritional Analysis: 2 stuffed pepper halves equals 317 calories, 12 g fat (4 g saturated fat), 56 mg cholesterol, 1,250 mg sodium, 24 g carbohydrate, 6 g fiber, 25 g protein.

Simple Stuffed Peppers

Traditional stuffed peppers call for cutting the tops off the peppers, seeding and stuffing. With this fast variation, you cut the peppers in half, making it easier to remove the seeds and to stuff.

Time-Saving Tip

Cook the rice the night before, cool and refrigerate in a covered container. There's no need to reheat before adding to the meat mixture.

Fruit 'n' Nut Chili

PREP: 10 min.   **COOK:** 30 min.

1-1/2 pounds ground beef
   1 cup chopped onion
   1 cup chopped green pepper
   1 teaspoon minced garlic
   1 can (28 ounces) crushed tomatoes
   2 cups water
   2 cups chopped peeled apples
   1 can (15-1/2 ounces) chili beans, undrained
   1 can (6 ounces) tomato paste
 1/3 cup slivered almonds
   2 tablespoons baking cocoa
   2 tablespoons chili powder
   1 teaspoon salt
   1 teaspoon ground cinnamon
   1 teaspoon pepper
Sour cream, optional

In a Dutch oven, cook the beef, onion, green pepper and garlic over medium heat until meat is no longer pink; drain. Stir in the tomatoes, water, apples, beans, tomato paste, almonds, cocoa and seasonings.

Bring to a boil. Reduce heat; cover and simmer for 30 minutes or until heated through. Garnish with sour cream if desired.

Yield: 7 servings.

Nutritional Analysis: *1-1/2 cups equals 340 calories, 13 g fat (4 g saturated fat), 48 mg cholesterol, 773 mg sodium, 37 g carbohydrate, 10 g fiber, 25 g protein.*

Chili Choices

There are as many variations of chili as there are cooks making it! The addition of cocoa in this rich version makes it similar to Cincinnati-style chili.

Serving Suggestion

Dish out hearty helpings of chili in bread bowls. Any large, firm-textured rolls from the bakery will do. Cut off the top, scoop out some bread and fill with chili. Serve the tops on the side for dipping.

Italian Stew

1 pound ground beef
1/2 pound bulk mild Italian sausage
1 cup chopped onion
1 can (15 ounces) cannellini *or* white kidney beans, rinsed and drained
2 cups cut fresh green beans
1 can (14-1/2 ounces) Italian stewed tomatoes
1 cup vegetable broth
1 can (6 ounces) tomato paste
2 teaspoons dried oregano
1 teaspoon salt
1/2 teaspoon pepper
1 bunch escarole, trimmed and torn
1/2 cup shredded Parmesan cheese

In a large skillet or Dutch oven, cook the beef, sausage and onion over medium heat until meat is no longer pink; drain. Add cannellini and green beans, tomatoes, broth, tomato paste, oregano, salt and pepper.

Bring to a boil. Reduce heat; cover and simmer for 15 minutes. Add escarole; cover and simmer 5 minutes longer or until escarole is wilted. Sprinkle with Parmesan cheese.

Yield: 6 servings.

Nutritional Analysis: 1-1/2 cups equals 339 calories, 14 g fat (6 g saturated fat), 57 mg cholesterol, 1,252 mg sodium, 28 g carbohydrate, 9 g fiber, 26 g protein.

Escarole Education

Escarole, a salad green of the chicory family, has broad, wavy jagged-edged green outer leaves that whiten near the core. Wash each leaf well, pat dry and trim off the white core.

Lively Leftover

If you purchase bulk mild Italian sausage in a 1-pound package, freeze half in a resealable plastic bag to make Sausage Polenta Bake on page 164 at a later date.

Blues Burgers

PREP: 10 min.   **GRILL:** 15 min.

1/2 pound sliced fresh mushrooms
2 tablespoons butter
1-1/2 pounds lean ground beef
1/2 teaspoon ground cumin
1/2 teaspoon paprika
1/4 teaspoon salt
1/4 teaspoon chili powder
1/4 teaspoon pepper
Pinch cayenne pepper
2 ounces crumbled blue cheese
2/3 cup barbecue sauce
4 onion rolls *or* hamburger buns, split

Better Grilled Burgers

To keep burgers moist and juicy, never flatten them with a spatula while grilling. This squeezes out the tasty juices and flavor.

Substitution Secret

Not a fan of blue cheese? Use shredded Swiss, mozzarella, Monterey Jack or cheddar instead.

In a skillet, saute mushrooms in butter for 2-3 minutes or until tender. Set aside and keep warm.

In a bowl, combine the beef and seasonings just until mixed. Shape into eight thin patties. Sprinkle half of the patties with blue cheese; top with remaining patties and press edges firmly to seal.

Grill, uncovered, over medium-hot heat for 3 minutes on each side. Brush with some of the barbecue sauce. Grill 10-12 minutes longer or until juices run clear, brushing with sauce and turning occasionally. Drain mushrooms. Serve burgers on rolls topped with mushrooms.

Yield: 4 servings.

Nutritional Analysis: 1 burger equals 552 calories, 26 g fat (13 g saturated fat), 109 mg cholesterol, 1,128 mg sodium, 34 g carbohydrate, 2 g fiber, 43 g protein.

14

Zippy Beef Bake

PREP: 15 min.   **BAKE:** 20 min.

3/4   pound ground beef
1   tablespoon butter
2   medium zucchini, thinly sliced
1/4   pound sliced fresh mushrooms
2   tablespoons sliced green onions
1-1/2   teaspoons chili powder
1   teaspoon salt
1/8   teaspoon garlic powder
1-1/2   cups cooked rice
1   can (4 ounces) chopped green chilies
1/2   cup sour cream
1   cup (4 ounces) shredded Monterey Jack cheese,
    divided

Preparation Pointer

To get the 1-1/2 cups of cooked rice called for in this recipe, start with 1/2 cup of uncooked long grain white rice.

Substitution Secret

Sliced yellow squash can be substituted for the zucchini in this casserole.

In a large skillet, cook beef over medium heat until no longer pink; drain. Add the butter, zucchini, mushrooms and onions. Cook and stir until vegetables are tender; drain.

Stir in the chili powder, salt and garlic powder. Add the rice, chilies, sour cream and 1/2 cup cheese. Transfer to a greased 2-qt. baking dish; sprinkle with remaining cheese. Bake, uncovered, at 350° for 20-22 minutes or until cheese is melted.

Yield: 4 servings.

Nutritional Analysis: 1 cup equals 462 calories, 27 g fat (15 g saturated fat), 109 mg cholesterol, 944 mg sodium, 23 g carbohydrate, 2 g fiber, 29 g protein.

Speedy **Ground Beef**

Beef Tostadas

PREP/TOTAL TIME: 15 min.

1 pound lean ground beef
1 cup chopped sweet red pepper
1/2 cup chili sauce
1 teaspoon Mexican *or* taco seasoning
1/4 teaspoon salt
1/4 teaspoon pepper
1/2 cup sour cream
3 teaspoons chipotle sauce
6 tostada shells
3 cups shredded lettuce
1-1/2 cups guacamole
1-1/2 cups shredded Mexican cheese blend

In a large skillet, cook beef and red pepper over medium heat until meat is no longer pink; drain. Stir in the chili sauce, Mexican seasoning, salt and pepper; heat through.

In a small bowl, combine the sour cream and chipotle sauce. Layer each tostada with lettuce, meat mixture, guacamole, cheese and chipotle cream.

Yield: 6 servings.

Nutritional Analysis: 1 tostada equals 460 calories, 30 g fat (13 g saturated fat), 75 mg cholesterol, 1,040 mg sodium, 22 g carbohydrate, 6 g fiber, 24 g protein.

Preparation Pointer

Look for prepared guacamole in your grocery store's produce area. Guacamole dip, found in the dairy section, can be substituted but has a thinner consistency.

Substitution Secret

The beef filling can also be used with flour tortillas to make soft-shell tacos or burritos. Or roll up the flour tortillas, top with a can of enchilada sauce and bake for easy enchiladas.

Crescent Beef Casserole

PREP/TOTAL TIME: 30 min.

1   pound lean ground beef
1   cup diced zucchini
1/4   cup chopped onion
1/4   cup chopped green pepper
2   teaspoons olive oil
1   cup tomato puree
1   teaspoon dried oregano
1/4   teaspoon salt
1/8   teaspoon pepper
1-1/2   cups mashed potatoes
1   cup (4 ounces) crumbled feta cheese
1   tube (8 ounces) refrigerated crescent rolls

In a large skillet, cook beef over medium heat until no longer pink; drain and set aside. In the same skillet, saute the zucchini, onion and green pepper in oil until crisp-tender. Stir in the beef, tomato puree, oregano, salt and pepper; heat through.

Spread mashed potatoes in an 11-in. x 7-in. x 2-in. baking dish coated with nonstick cooking spray. Top with beef mixture; sprinkle with feta cheese.

Unroll crescent dough. Separate into four rectangles; arrange three rectangles over the casserole. Bake at 375° for 12-15 minutes or until top is browned. Roll remaining dough into two crescent rolls; bake for another use.

Yield: 6 servings.

Nutritional Analysis: 1 serving equals 442 calories, 22 g fat (9 g saturated fat), 67 mg cholesterol, 938 mg sodium, 30 g carbohydrate, 2 g fiber, 26 g protein.

Preparation Pointer

Instead of chopping onion and green pepper every time you need them, try this trick.

After chopping, freeze in a single layer on a large baking sheet. When frozen, transfer to separate heavy-duty resealable plastic bags. It's easy to measure out just what you need for each recipe. And because they cook quickly, there's no need to defrost first.

Asparagus Beef Stir-Fry

PREP/TOTAL TIME: 25 min.

1 pound lean ground beef
2 cups cut fresh asparagus (1-inch pieces)
1 can (8 ounces) sliced water chestnuts, drained
1 package (5 ounces) sliced fresh shiitake mushrooms
1 teaspoon minced garlic
2 teaspoons sesame oil
2 tablespoons cornstarch
1-1/2 cups beef broth
1/3 cup hoisin sauce
2 tablespoons reduced-sodium soy sauce
1 teaspoon minced fresh gingerroot
1 large tomato, chopped
Hot cooked rice, optional

Give Gingerroot A Try!

Fresh gingerroot is available in the produce section of most major grocery stores. Select gingerroot with a smooth skin—if wrinkled or cracked, it's past its prime.

When stored in a heavy-duty resealable plastic bag, unpeeled gingerroot can be frozen for up to 1 year. When needed for a recipe, simply peel and grate.

In a large skillet or wok, cook beef over medium heat until no longer pink; drain and set aside. In the same pan, stir-fry the asparagus, water chestnuts, mushrooms and garlic in oil for 5 minutes or until crisp-tender.

In a small bowl, combine the cornstarch, broth, hoisin sauce, soy sauce and ginger until blended; pour over vegetables. Return beef to the pan. Bring to a boil; cook and stir for 2 minutes or until thickened. Remove from the heat; stir in the tomato. Serve with rice if desired.

Yield: 4 servings.

Nutritional Analysis: 1 cup beef mixture (calculated without rice) equals 338 calories, 12 g fat (4 g saturated fat), 56 mg cholesterol, 1,040 mg sodium, 31 g carbohydrate, 5 g fiber, 27 g protein.

Hominy Beef Polenta

PREP/TOTAL TIME: 30 min.

2 packages (1 pound *each*) polenta, cut into 1/2-inch slices
1 pound ground beef
1 cup chopped sweet red pepper
1 jar (16 ounces) picante sauce
1 can (15-1/2 ounces) hot chili beans, undrained
1 can (15-1/2 ounces) hominy, rinsed and drained
1/3 cup minced fresh cilantro
3 teaspoons ground cumin
2 teaspoons chili powder
2 cups (8 ounces) shredded Colby-Monterey Jack cheese

Line a greased 13-in. x 9-in. x 2-in. baking dish with a single layer of polenta slices. Bake, uncovered, at 350° for 15-20 minutes or until heated through.

Meanwhile, in a large skillet, cook beef and red pepper over medium heat until meat is no longer pink; drain. Stir in the picante sauce, beans, hominy, cilantro, cumin and chili powder; heat through.

Sprinkle half of the cheese over polenta. Top with meat sauce and remaining cheese. Bake for 8 minutes or until cheese is melted.

Yield: 6 servings.

Nutritional Analysis: 1 cup equals 503 calories, 18 g fat (11 g saturated fat), 72 mg cholesterol, 1,865 mg sodium, 52 g carbohydrate, 8 g fiber, 28 g protein.

Cilantro Substitution

With its slightly sharp flavor, cilantro gives foods a distinct taste. If you and your family don't care for the taste, simply use parsley instead.

A Polenta Lesson

Polenta can be found either in the refrigerated produce department or the Italian section of your grocery store.

Let polenta liven up your breakfasts! Pick up a package and bake as directed. Cut into squares and top with scrambled eggs, salsa and shredded cheese.

Ground Beef a la King

PREP/TOTAL TIME: 30 min.

1 package (10 ounces) frozen puff pastry shells
1 package (16 ounces) fresh baby carrots, cut in half
1-1/4 cups water, *divided*
1-1/2 pounds lean ground beef
1 package (8 ounces) sliced baby portobello mushrooms
2 tablespoons chopped shallots
3 tablespoons all-purpose flour
1 can (10-1/2 ounces) condensed beef broth, undiluted
1/4 cup tomato paste
1/4 cup dry red wine
1 tablespoon minced fresh tarragon
1/2 teaspoon salt
1/4 teaspoon pepper

Bake pastry shells according to package directions. In a microwave-safe bowl, combine the carrots and 1 cup of water. Cover and microwave on high for 8-10 minutes or until crisp-tender. Meanwhile, in a large skillet, cook the beef, mushrooms and shallots over medium heat until meat is no longer pink; drain. Combine the flour and broth until smooth. Add the broth mixture, tomato paste, wine, tarragon, salt, pepper and remaining water to beef mixture; stir to combine.

Drain carrots; add to skillet. Bring to a boil. Reduce heat; cover and simmer for 15 minutes. Remove top of pastry shells; fill with beef mixture.

Editor's Note: This recipe was tested in a 1,100-watt microwave.

Yield: 6 servings.

Nutritional Analysis: 1-1/4 cups beef mixture with one pastry shell equals 481 calories, 23 g fat (6 g saturated fat), 56 mg cholesterol, 836 mg sodium, 37 g carbohydrate, 6 g fiber, 29 g protein.

Substitution Secret

Pass on the puff pastry shells next time you make this dish and serve the ground beef mixture over refrigerated mashed potatoes, hot cooked pasta or refrigerated biscuits.

Southwestern Skillet Burgers

PREP/TOTAL TIME: 30 min.

> 2 pounds ground beef
> 1/2 cup dry bread crumbs
> 1 envelope taco seasoning
> 1 can (14-1/2 ounces) diced tomatoes with onions, undrained
> 1 can (11-1/2 ounces) condensed bean with bacon soup, undiluted
> 1/2 cup shredded cheddar cheese

In a bowl, combine the beef, bread crumbs and taco seasoning. Shape into six 3/4-in.-thick patties. In a large skillet over medium heat, cook patties for 3 minutes on each side or until browned. Remove patties; drain.

Add tomatoes and soup to the skillet; return patties to the pan. Bring to a boil. Reduce heat; cover and simmer for 10 minutes or until meat is no longer pink. Sprinkle with cheese; cover and heat until cheese is melted.

Yield: 6 servings.

Nutritional Analysis: 1 patty with 1/2 cup tomato mixture equals 483 calories, 23 g fat (10 g saturated fat), 125 mg cholesterol, 945 mg sodium, 17 g carbohydrate, 1 g fiber, 36 g protein.

Quick Corn On the Cob

These stovetop burgers need only a simple side dish to make a mouth-watering meal. Here's a quick way to make corn on the cob.

Place 6 small ears of fresh corn on the cob in a Dutch oven of boiling water. Cook for 3-5 minutes or until tender; drain. Top with butter and season to taste with salt and pepper.

Meaty Whole Grain Nachos

PREP/TOTAL TIME: 20 min.

1/2 pound lean ground beef
1/2 pound uncooked chorizo sausage
1/2 cup chopped green pepper
1/4 cup chopped onion
1 can (16 ounces) baked beans
1 jar (8 ounces) salsa
1/4 cup barbecue sauce
1/2 cup shredded cheddar cheese
1 package (13-1/2 ounces) multigrain snack chips
Shredded lettuce, chopped tomatoes and chopped green
    onions, optional

In a large skillet, cook the beef, sausage, green pepper and onion over medium heat until meat is no longer pink; drain. Stir in the beans, salsa and barbecue sauce; heat through. Sprinkle with cheese. Use snack chips for dipping. Serve with lettuce, tomatoes and green onions if desired.

Yield: 8 servings.

Nutritional Analysis: 1/2 cup beef mixture with 1 cup chips equals 1,025 calories, 52 g fat (15 g saturated fat), 101 mg cholesterol, 2,072 mg sodium, 98 g carbohydrate, 17 g fiber, 44 g protein.

Why Chose Chorizo?

Chorizo sausage is a seasoned, smoked pork sausage flavored with garlic, chili powder and other spices. It's widely used in Spanish cooking. If you don't see it in your grocery's meat case, ask the butcher.

Serving Suggestion

If you can't find disposable nacho chip containers like those pictured, give each person a small bowl of the meat mixture and serve the snack chips on the side.

Speedy **Ground Beef**

Pesto Hamburgers

PREP/TOTAL TIME: 20 min.

1-1/2	pounds ground beef
1/8	teaspoon salt
1/8	teaspoon pepper
4	slices mozzarella cheese
1/2	cup prepared pesto
1/3	cup roasted sweet red pepper strips
4	hamburger buns, split and toasted

Shape beef into four 3/4-in.-thick patties. Season with salt and pepper. In a large skillet over medium heat, cook patties for 5 minutes on each side or until meat is no longer pink. Top each burger with cheese, 2 tablespoons pesto and pepper strips. Reduce heat; cover and simmer for 2 minutes or until cheese is melted. Serve on buns.

Yield: 4 servings.

Nutritional Analysis: 1 burger equals 716 calories, 45 g fat (17 g saturated fat), 161 mg cholesterol, 779 mg sodium, 25 g carbohydrate, 2 g fiber, 51 g protein.

Homemade Pesto

When your basil plant is full and bushy, make a batch of homemade pesto. Use to top grilled meats or toss with hot cooked pasta.

For 3/4 cup pesto, place 1 cup lightly packed fresh basil leaves, 1 cup tightly packed fresh parsley leaves, 1 to 2 peeled garlic cloves, 1/2 cup olive oil, 1/2 cup grated Parmesan cheese and 1/4 teaspoon salt in a food processor. Cover and process on high until pureed. Refrigerate for several weeks or freeze in 1/4 cup portions for up to 6 months.

Substitution Secret

Instead of making the hamburgers from scratch, pick up a package of pre-shaped patties in the meat section of your grocery store. Or keep frozen hamburger patties on hand when you have the hankering for a hamburger but little time to cook from scratch.

Individual Greek Pizzas

PREP/TOTAL TIME: 30 min.

    1   package (5 ounces) fresh baby spinach
    1   tablespoon olive oil
  1/2   pound lean ground beef
    1   can (15 ounces) pizza sauce
    2   packages (10 ounces *each*) prebaked mini Italian
        bread shell crusts
    4   plum tomatoes, sliced
    1   cup crumbled tomato and basil feta cheese
  1/4   cup pine nuts, toasted

In a large skillet, saute spinach in oil for 2-3 minutes or until wilted; set aside. In the same skillet, cook beef over medium heat until no longer pink; drain. Stir in pizza sauce; cook for 5 minutes or until heated through.

Place crusts in an ungreased 15-in. x 10-in. x 1-in. baking pan; spread with meat sauce to within 1/2 in. of edges. Layer with spinach, tomatoes, feta cheese and pine nuts. Bake at 450° for 8-10 minutes or until cheese is melted.

Yield: 4 servings.

Nutritional Analysis: 1 pizza equals 687 calories, 27 g fat (8 g saturated fat), 43 mg cholesterol, 1,436 mg sodium, 77 g carbohydrate, 7 g fiber, 35 g protein.

Preparation Pointer

Cooking the frozen spinach in oil eliminates the need to squeeze the water from the leaves and keeps your pizza sauce from becoming too watery.

Simple Snack Idea

Make this dish using one large Italian bread shell crust and serve it as a hearty appetizer.

Zucchini Lasagna

PREP: 5 min.   **COOK:** 55 min.

1   pound ground beef
1/2   cup chopped onion
2   jars (one 26 ounces, one 14 ounces)
     meatless spaghetti sauce
1   can (15 ounces) crushed tomatoes
1   teaspoon dried basil
1   teaspoon dried oregano
1   teaspoon fennel seed, crushed
1   teaspoon minced garlic
9   no-cook lasagna noodles
2   cups sliced zucchini
1   cup ricotta cheese
1   carton (5 ounces) shredded Asiago cheese

In a large skillet, cook beef and onion over medium heat until meat is no longer pink; drain. Stir in the spaghetti sauce, tomatoes, basil, oregano, fennel and garlic. Bring to a boil. Reduce heat; cover and simmer for 10 minutes.

Spread 1-1/2 cups meat sauce in a greased 13-in. x 9-in. x 2-in. baking dish. Top with three noodles. Spread 1-1/2 cups sauce to edges of noodles. Top with half of the zucchini, 1/2 cup ricotta cheese and 1/2 cup Asiago cheese. Repeat layers. Top with remaining noodles, sauce and Asiago cheese.

Cover and bake at 375° for 30 minutes. Uncover; bake 10-15 minutes more or until bubbly. Let stand 5 minutes before cutting.

Yield: 6 servings.

Nutritional Analysis: 1 piece equals 495 calories, 18 g fat (10 g saturated fat), 75 mg cholesterol, 797 mg sodium, 50 g carbohydrate, 6 g fiber, 33 g protein.

All About Asiago

Asiago cheese is used extensively in Italian cooking. The color of the cheese changes from a creamy shade of white to a pale straw color as it ages, and the sweet flavor intensifies with time.

Preparation Pointer

No-cook noodles save prep time for this lasagna recipe. Since the noodles will expand during baking, avoid overlapping them. The noodles will touch the sides of dish upon baking.

Tropical Beef and Noodles

PREP/TOTAL TIME: 25 min.

- 4 cups uncooked egg noodles
- 1 pound ground beef
- 1 can (15 ounces) mandarin oranges
- 1 can (8 ounces) unsweetened pineapple chunks
- 2 tablespoons cornstarch
- 1 tablespoon lemon juice
- 1 tablespoon soy sauce
- 1/4 teaspoon garlic powder
- 1/4 teaspoon salt
- 1/8 teaspoon ground nutmeg
- 1/3 cup salted whole cashews
- 1/3 cup flaked coconut, toasted

Cook noodles according to package directions. Meanwhile, in a large skillet, cook beef over medium heat until no longer pink; drain.

Drain the mandarin oranges and pineapple, reserving juices. Set fruit aside. In a bowl, whisk the cornstarch and reserved juices until smooth; stir in the lemon juice, soy sauce, garlic powder, salt and nutmeg. Pour over beef.

Bring to a boil; cook and stir for 2 minutes or until thickened. Stir in the cashews, oranges and pineapple. Cook for 2 minutes or until heated through. Drain noodles; top with beef mixture. Sprinkle with coconut.

Yield: 4 servings.

Nutritional Analysis: 1 cup beef mixture with 1 cup noodles equals 528 calories, 21 g fat (9 g saturated fat), 92 mg cholesterol, 569 mg sodium, 54 g carbohydrate, 3 g fiber, 29 g protein.

Substitution Secret

Any kind of pasta or rice can be used in place of the egg noodles in this recipe.

Toasting Coconut

To toast coconut, spread in a single layer on a baking sheet with shallow sides. Bake at 325° for about 10 minutes or until golden brown, stirring often. Be sure to watch carefully so it doesn't burn.

Santa Fe Enchiladas

PREP/TOTAL TIME: 25 min.

1-1/2   pounds lean ground beef
   1   medium onion, chopped
   1   can (12 ounces) tomato paste
   1   cup water
   1   envelope taco seasoning
 10   flour tortillas (6 inches), warmed
   1   jar (8 ounces) process cheese sauce
   1   can (4 ounces) chopped green chilies

Crumble beef into a large microwave-safe bowl; stir in onion. Cover and microwave on high for 4-1/2 to 6 minutes or until meat is no longer pink, stirring every 1-1/2 minutes; drain. Stir in the tomato paste, water and taco seasoning. Cover and cook on high for 2-3 minutes or until heated through, stirring once.

Spoon about 1/3 cup meat mixture down the center of each tortilla; roll up tightly. Place seam side down in a greased shallow 2-1/2-qt. microwave-safe dish. Set remaining meat mixture aside. In a microwave-safe bowl, combine cheese sauce and chilies. Cover and microwave on high for 50 seconds; stir. Pour over tortillas.

Spoon remaining meat mixture down the center of tortillas. Cover and cook on high for 4 to 4-1/2 minutes or until heated through. Let stand for 5 minutes before serving.

Editor's Note: This recipe was tested in a 1,100-watt microwave.

Yield: 5 servings.

Nutritional Analysis: 2 enchiladas equals 609 calories, 25 g fat (11 g saturated fat), 94 mg cholesterol, 2,081 mg sodium, 54 g carbohydrate, 5 g fiber, 40 g protein.

Freezing Ground Beef

Ground beef is a great ingredient to have on hand for fast meals. Place uncooked ground beef in a heavy-duty resealable plastic bag; freeze and use within 3 months.

Ground beef wrapped and frozen flat will stack easily and make the best use of freezer space. These packages also thaw faster.

Serving Suggestion

If you're looking for a way to sneak more vegetables into your meals, chop up some tomatoes and Romaine lettuce; sprinkle over the top of these enchiladas just before serving.

Taco Puffs

PREP/TOTAL TIME: 30 min.

> 1   **pound ground beef**
> 1/2   **cup chopped onion**
> 1   **envelope taco seasoning**
> 2   **tubes (16.3 ounces *each*) large refrigerated flaky biscuits**
> 8   **ounces cheddar cheese slices *or* 2 cups (8 ounces) shredded cheddar cheese**

In a large skillet, cook beef and onion over medium heat until meat is no longer pink; drain. Add the taco seasoning and prepare according to package directions. Cool slightly.

Flatten half of the biscuits into 4-in. circles; place in greased 15-in. x 10-in. x 1-in. baking pans. Spoon 1/4 cup meat mixture onto each; top with two cheese slices or 1/4 cup shredded cheese. Flatten the remaining biscuits; place on top and pinch edges to seal tightly. Bake at 400° for 15 minutes or until golden brown.

Yield: 8 servings.

Nutritional Analysis: 1 puff equals 646 calories, 34 g fat (13 g saturated fat), 67 mg cholesterol, 1,775 mg sodium, 55 g carbohydrate, 2 g fiber, 26 g protein.

Preparation Pointer

If your family favors Mexican food, consider having taco meat ready to go in the freezer.

Cook 3 pounds ground beef and 1-1/2 cups chopped onion over medium heat until meat is no longer pink; drain. Add 3 envelopes taco seasoning and prepare according to package directions. Cool and freeze in 1-pound portions.

Hobo Meatball Stew

PREP: 20 min.   **COOK:** 4 hours

1	pound ground beef
1-1/2	teaspoons salt, *divided*
1/2	teaspoon pepper, *divided*
4	medium potatoes, peeled and cut into chunks
4	medium carrots, cut into chunks
1	large onion, cut into chunks
1/2	cup water
1/2	cup ketchup
1-1/2	teaspoons cider vinegar
1/2	teaspoon dried basil

In a bowl, combine the beef, 1 teaspoon salt and 1/4 teaspoon pepper. Shape into 1-in. balls. In a skillet over medium heat, brown meatballs on all sides; drain.

Place the potatoes, carrots and onion in a 3-qt. slow cooker; top with meatballs. Combine the water, ketchup, vinegar, basil, and remaining salt and pepper; pour over meatballs. Cover and cook on high for 4-5 hours or until the vegetables are tender.

Yield: 4 servings.

Nutritional Analysis: 1-1/2 cups equals 402 calories, 14 g fat (6 g saturated fat), 75 mg cholesterol, 1,324 mg sodium, 43 g carbohydrate, 5 g fiber, 26 g protein.

Potato Tips

If stored in a cool, dark place, potatoes will remain fresh for nearly 2 weeks, so they're a great staple to have on hand. Any kind of potato can be used in this recipe. Experiment with russet (or Idaho), round, red, new, white and Yukon Gold varieties.

Substitution Secret

Instead of making meatballs from scratch, substitute 1 pound of frozen fully cooked meatballs. There's no need to thaw before putting them in the slow cooker.

Corn Bread Sloppy Joes

PREP/TOTAL TIME: 30 min.

 1 package (8-1/2 ounces) corn bread/muffin mix
 1 egg
 1/3 cup milk
 2 pounds ground beef
 1/2 cup chopped onion
 1 jar (26 ounces) meatless spaghetti sauce
 1 cup frozen corn
 1 can (4 ounces) chopped green chilies, drained
 2 envelopes sloppy joe mix
 1 cup (4 ounces) shredded cheddar cheese

Prepare and bake corn bread according to package directions, using the egg and milk. Meanwhile, in a large skillet, cook beef and onion over medium heat until meat is no longer pink; drain. Stir in the spaghetti sauce, corn, chilies and sloppy joe mix. Bring to a boil. Reduce heat; simmer, uncovered, for 10 minutes.

Sprinkle with cheese; cover and cook for 1 minute or until cheese is melted. Cut corn bread into six pieces; cut each piece in half. Top with sloppy joe mixture.

Yield: 6 servings.

Nutritional Analysis: 1 cup sloppy joe mixture with 2 pieces of corn bread equals 592 calories, 25 g fat (12 g saturated fat), 142 mg cholesterol, 1,658 mg sodium, 54 g carbohydrate, 4 g fiber, 38 g protein.

Substitution Secret

Instead of making a pan of corn bread from scratch, you can purchase ready-to-eat corn bread from your grocer's bakery department.

Time-Saving Tip

For an even faster recipe, cook the beef and onion; drain. Instead of using spaghetti sauce and sloppy joe mix, add two cans (15-1/2 ounces *each*) sloppy joe sauce to the skillet; cook according to the package directions. Stir in the corn and chilies; sprinkle with cheese. Serve over slices of purchased corn bread.

Speedy **Ground Beef**

Sicilian Spaghetti Sauce

PREP/TOTAL TIME: 30 min.

1/2	pound lean ground beef
1/2	cup chopped onion
1	teaspoon minced garlic
1	teaspoon olive oil
2	cans (14-1/2 ounces *each*) Italian diced tomatoes, undrained
1/4	cup golden raisins
1/4	cup dry red wine
2	tablespoons tomato paste
1	tablespoon sugar
1	teaspoon dried basil
1/2	teaspoon salt
1/4	teaspoon pepper
8	ounces uncooked spaghetti
2	tablespoons minced fresh parsley
2	teaspoons pine nuts, toasted

In a large skillet, cook the beef, onion and garlic in oil over medium heat until meat is no longer pink; drain. Stir in the tomatoes, raisins, wine, tomato paste, sugar, basil, salt and pepper. Bring to a boil. Reduce heat; simmer, uncovered, for 15 minutes or until heated through.

Meanwhile, cook spaghetti according to package directions. Stir parsley and pine nuts into meat sauce. Drain spaghetti; top with sauce.

Yield: 4 servings.

Nutritional Analysis: 1 cup sauce with 1 cup spaghetti equals 457 calories, 7 g fat (2 g saturated fat), 28 mg cholesterol, 1,138 mg sodium, 74 g carbohydrate, 4 g fiber, 21 g protein.

Lively Leftovers

Make a double batch of Sicilian Spaghetti Sauce and freeze half for a quick meal later on. Or refrigerate leftovers for dinner the next night.

Toasting Pine Nuts

Toast the pine nuts while the spaghetti sauce is simmering. Place nuts in a small skillet over medium heat. Stir frequently until golden brown. Be sure to watch carefully because they can brown quickly.

Hamburger Minestrone

PREP/TOTAL TIME: 30 min.

1/2 cup small uncooked pasta shells
  1 pound ground beef
1/2 cup chopped onion
  3 cans (14-1/2 ounces *each*) beef broth
  1 package (16 ounces) frozen mixed vegetables
  1 can (16 ounces) kidney beans, rinsed and drained
  1 can (14-1/2 ounces) diced tomatoes, undrained
  1 can (6 ounces) tomato paste
  3 teaspoons Italian seasoning
  1 teaspoon salt
1/4 teaspoon dried thyme
1/4 teaspoon dried basil
1/4 teaspoon pepper

Cook pasta according to package directions. Meanwhile, in a soup kettle or large saucepan, cook beef and onion over medium heat until meat is no longer pink; drain.

Stir in the remaining ingredients. Bring to a boil. Reduce heat; simmer, uncovered, for 15 minutes. Drain pasta and add to the pan. Cook 5 minutes longer or until heated through.

Yield: 6 servings.

Nutritional Analysis: 1-1/2 cups equals 324 calories, 8 g fat (4 g saturated fat), 37 mg cholesterol, 1,427 mg sodium, 40 g carbohydrate, 10 g fiber, 25 g protein.

Lively Leftover

Double the recipe for Hamburger Minestrone Soup. Before adding pasta to the pan, freeze half of the soup in individual-size portions. Thaw and add cooked pasta for a quick lunch or dinner for one.

Substitution Secret

Replace the basic frozen mixed vegetables with any other frozen varieties, such as sugar snap stir-fry (with sugar snap peas, carrots, onions and mushrooms) or frozen vegetables for stew.

You don't have to wait for the weekend to cook beef. These recipes use quick-cooking cuts for hearty meals in minutes!

Steaks with Chipotle Sauce (p. 64)

42

Quick & Easy **Beef**

Vegetable Beef Ragout

PREP/TOTAL TIME: 20 min.

   1 **cup sliced fresh mushrooms**
1/2 **cup chopped onion**
   1 **tablespoon vegetable oil**
   1 **package (17 ounces) refrigerated beef tips with gravy**
   1 **package (14 ounces) frozen sugar snap peas, thawed**
   1 **cup cherry tomatoes, halved**
Hot cooked pasta, optional

In a large skillet, saute mushrooms and onion in oil until tender. Add the beef tips with gravy, peas and tomatoes; heat through. Serve over pasta if desired.

Yield: 4 servings.

Nutritional Analysis: 1 cup beef mixture (calculated without noodles) equals 246 calories, 10 g fat (3 g saturated fat), 47 mg cholesterol, 670 mg sodium, 15 g carbohydrate, 4 g fiber, 21 g protein.

Preparation Pointer

Refrigerated beef tips with gravy can be found in the meat section of your grocery store. Reheat according to package directions and serve over refrigerated mashed potatoes.

Better yet, jazz up the beef tips by following this tasty recipe!

What Is Ragout?

Ragout (ra-GOO), a French word meaning "stew," is usually made of meat or poultry and a thick sauce.

Gingered Pepper Steak

PREP/TOTAL TIME: 25 min.

  2 teaspoons sugar
  2 teaspoons cornstarch
1/4 teaspoon ground ginger
1/4 cup reduced-sodium soy sauce
  1 tablespoon white wine vinegar
  1 pound beef flank steak, thinly sliced
  2 medium green peppers, julienned
  1 teaspoon vegetable oil
Hot cooked rice, optional

In a large bowl, combine the sugar, cornstarch, ginger, soy sauce and vinegar until smooth. Add beef and toss to coat; set aside.

In a large skillet or wok, stir-fry the green peppers in oil until crisp-tender, about 3 minutes. Remove with a slotted spoon and keep warm. Add the beef with marinade to pan; stir-fry for 3 minutes or until meat reaches desired doneness. Return peppers to pan; heat through. Serve over rice if desired.

Yield: 4 servings.

Nutritional Analysis: 1 cup beef mixture (calculated without rice) equals 218 calories, 9 g fat (4 g saturated fat), 54 mg cholesterol, 674 mg sodium, 8 g carbohydrate, 1 g fiber, 23 g protein.

Slice Steak Faster

It will be easier to thinly slice the flank steak while it's still partially frozen. Plus, the slices will thaw faster than one large piece.

Speedy Side Dish

Instant rice is all you need to round out this stir-fry supper. It's the perfect accompaniment because it cooks in mere minutes.

Seasoned Short Ribs

PREP: 15 min.   **COOK:** 6 hours

- 1-1/2 cups tomato juice
- 1/2 cup maple syrup
- 1/4 cup chopped onion
- 3 tablespoons cider vinegar
- 1 tablespoon Worcestershire sauce
- 1 tablespoon Dijon mustard
- 2 teaspoons minced garlic
- 1/4 teaspoon ground cinnamon
- 1/4 teaspoon ground cloves
- 4 pounds bone-in beef short ribs
- 1 teaspoon pepper
- 1 tablespoon cornstarch
- 2 tablespoons cold water

Sweet Potatoes 'n' Pears
(p. 277)

In a small bowl, combine the first nine ingredients; set aside. Cut ribs into serving-size pieces; place on a broiler pan. Sprinkle with pepper. Broil 4-6 in. from the heat for 3-5 minutes on each side or until browned; drain on paper towels.

Place ribs in a 5-qt. slow cooker; top with tomato juice mixture. Cover and cook on low for 6-7 hours or until meat is tender.

In a small bowl, combine cornstarch and cold water until smooth. Pour 1 cup cooking liquid into a small saucepan; skim off fat. Bring to a boil; stir in cornstarch mixture. Return to a boil; cook and stir for 2 minutes or until thickened. Serve over ribs.

Yield: 4 servings.

Nutritional Analysis: 2 ribs equals 1,169 calories, 92 g fat (39 g saturated fat), 206 mg cholesterol, 538 mg sodium, 34 g carbohydrate, 1 g fiber, 48 g protein.

Foil Means Fast Cleanup

For faster cleanup, line your broiler pan with heavy-duty aluminum foil before broiling the beef short ribs.

Speedy Side Dish

A special side dish like Sweet Potatoes 'n' Pears pairs well with Seasoned Short Ribs. You'll find the recipe on page 277.

Grilled Rib Eyes

PREP: 10 min. + marinating   **GRILL:** 10 min.

- 2   tablespoons brown sugar
- 1   tablespoon baking cocoa
- 1   tablespoon instant coffee granules, finely crushed
- 1   teaspoon paprika
- 1/2   teaspoon salt
- 1/2   teaspoon ground allspice
- 1/2   teaspoon pepper
- 4   boneless rib eye steaks (6 ounces *each*)

In a small bowl, combine the first seven ingredients. Rub over both sides of steaks. Refrigerate for 1 hour.

Grill steaks, uncovered, over medium-hot heat for 5-8 minutes on each side or until meat reaches desired doneness (for rare, a meat thermometer should read 140°; medium, 160°; well-done, 170°).

Yield: 4 servings.

Nutritional Analysis: 1 steak equals 409 calories, 27 g fat (11 g saturated fat), 101 mg cholesterol, 376 mg sodium, 9 g carbohydrate, 1 g fiber, 31 g protein.

Speedy Side Dish

What to pair with sizzling steaks hot off the grill? Nothing is easier than store-bought potato salad! And it's tasty, too.

Ways to Use the Rub

This rub can be used on a variety of beef cuts, including flank steak.

To cook a 1-1/2 pound flank steak, grill, covered, over medium-hot heat for 6-8 minutes on each side or until a meat thermometer reaches desired doneness. To serve, thinly slice across the grain.

Fillets with Plum Sauce

PREP/TOTAL TIME: 20 min.

> 4 beef tenderloin fillets (4 ounces *each*)
> 2 tablespoons butter
> 1/4 teaspoon salt
> 1/8 teaspoon pepper
> 2 medium plums, sliced
> 3 green onions, sliced
> 1/4 cup orange marmalade
> 2 tablespoons balsamic vinegar

In a large skillet over medium-high heat, cook fillets in butter until meat reaches desired doneness (for rare, a meat thermometer should read 140°; medium, 160°; well-done, 170°). Season with salt and pepper. Remove and keep warm.

In the same skillet, cook plums and onions for 2-3 minutes or until plums are tender. Add marmalade and vinegar; cook and stir until heated through. Serve over fillets.

Yield: 4 servings.

Nutritional Analysis: 1 serving equals 325 calories, 17 g fat (8 g saturated fat), 87 mg cholesterol, 273 mg sodium, 20 g carbohydrate, 1 g fiber, 24 g protein.

Purchasing Plums

Look for plums that give slightly to pressure. Avoid plums with cracks, soft spots or brown discoloration. A pale gray coating on the skin is natural and doesn't affect its quality. Refrigerate ripe plums in a plastic bag for up to 5 days.

Slicing Green Onions

To make quick work of slicing green onions, use a kitchen shears instead of a knife.

Moroccan Braised Beef

PREP: 20 min.   **COOK:** 7 hours

  1/3   cup all-purpose flour
    2   pounds boneless beef chuck roast, cut into 1-inch cubes
    3   tablespoons olive oil
    2   cans (14-1/2 ounces *each*) beef broth
    2   cups chopped onions
    1   can (14-1/2 ounces) diced tomatoes, undrained
    1   cup dry red wine
    1   tablespoon curry powder
    1   tablespoon paprika
    1   teaspoon salt
    1   teaspoon ground cumin
    1   teaspoon ground coriander
  1/2   teaspoon cayenne pepper
1-1/2   cups golden raisins
Hot cooked couscous, optional

Place flour in a large resealable plastic bag; add beef and toss to coat. In a large skillet, brown beef in oil. Transfer to a 5-qt. slow cooker. Stir in the broth, onions, tomatoes, wine and seasonings. Cover and cook on low for 7-8 hours or until the meat is tender.

During the last 30 minutes of cooking, stir in the raisins. Serve with couscous if desired.

Yield: 6 servings.

Nutritional Analysis: 1-1/3 cups beef mixture (calculated without couscous) equals 533 calories, 22 g fat (7 g saturated fat), 98 mg cholesterol, 620 mg sodium, 45 g carbohydrate, 5 g fiber, 34 g protein.

Curry Powder Primer

Curry powder is a blend of up to 20 spices, herbs and seeds. Add a pinch of curry to your favorite soups, stews, salads and even rice to add an exotic flavor.

In this recipe, begin by adding 2 teaspoons curry, then slowly add more to suit your taste.

Preparation Pointer

Moroccan Braised Beef can be prepared and frozen for future use. Be sure to store it in an airtight container and use within 2 months. When ready to eat, simply thaw and reheat.

52

Southwestern Beef Strips

PREP/TOTAL TIME: 20 min.

1-1/2	pounds boneless beef sirloin steak, cut into thin strips
1	medium onion, sliced
1	medium sweet red pepper, cut into thin strips
2	tablespoons Mexican seasoning
1	teaspoon salt
1/4	teaspoon pepper
2	tablespoons vegetable oil
1	can (15 ounces) black beans, rinsed and drained
1-1/2	cups frozen corn, thawed
1/2	cup picante sauce
2	teaspoons dried cilantro flakes

Hot cooked fettuccine, optional

In a large skillet, stir-fry the beef, onion, red pepper, Mexican seasoning, salt and pepper in oil until meat is no longer pink. Stir in the beans, corn, picante sauce and cilantro; heat through. Serve over fettuccine if desired.

Yield: 6 servings.

Nutritional Analysis: 1-1/3 cups beef mixture (calculated without fettuccine) equals 291 calories, 11 g fat (3 g saturated fat), 63 mg cholesterol, 777 mg sodium, 22 g carbohydrate, 5 g fiber, 27 g protein.

Pick the Right Picante!

Picante sauce comes in a variety of heat levels, which will affect the spiciness of Southwestern Beef Strips. Choose a variety that suits your family's taste.

Spicy Seasoning

Mexican seasoning is a blend of cumin, chili pepper, onion and garlic. It can be found in the spice section of your local grocery store. Keep some on hand and use to season ground beef or turkey for tasty tacos!

Pressure-Cooked Beef Stew

PREP: 15 min.   **COOK:** 50 min. + cooling

 1 boneless beef chuck roast (2 pounds)
 1 tablespoon vegetable oil
 5 cups water, *divided*
 8 medium potatoes, peeled and quartered
 4 medium carrots, halved widthwise
 1 medium onion, quartered
 1 teaspoon minced garlic
3/4 teaspoon salt
1/2 teaspoon pepper
1/2 teaspoon dried thyme
 2 bay leaves
 2 to 3 tablespoons cornstarch
1/4 cup cold water

In a pressure cooker, brown roast in oil on all sides. Remove roast. Add cooking rack; place roast on rack. Add 4 cups of water. Close cover securely; place pressure regulator on vent pipe. Bring cooker to full pressure over high heat. Reduce heat to medium-high; cook for 40 minutes. (Pressure regulator should maintain a slow steady rocking motion; adjust heat if needed.)

Remove from heat; allow pressure to drop on its own. Remove meat and keep warm. Pour pan juices into a bowl; skim fat. Remove rack from cooker. Add pan juices, remaining water and the next eight ingredients to cooker. Cover securely; return cooker to full pressure. Reduce heat; cook for 8 minutes. Immediately cool according to manufacturer's directions until pressure is completely reduced. With a slotted spoon, remove vegetables and keep warm. Discard bay leaves. Combine cornstarch and cold water until smooth; stir into pan juices. Bring to a boil; cook and stir for 2 minutes or until thickened. Serve with beef and vegetables.

Yield: 6 servings.

Nutritional Analysis: 1-1/2 cups equals 566 calories, 17 g fat (6 g saturated fat), 98 mg cholesterol, 391 mg sodium, 67 g carbohydrate, 7 g fiber, 36 g protein.

How a Pressure Cooker Works

Pressure cookers use pressurized steam to quickly cook foods. After the pressure cooker's lid is secured, the liquid inside begins boiling and produces steam. The trapped steam causes pressure to build and the temperature in the cooker to rise above the normal boiling point.

When the cooker reaches full pressure, the pressure regulator in the center of the lid starts to rock or jiggle. At this time, the heat is reduced just enough to maintain a slow rocking motion.

Reuben Slaw Sandwiches

PREP/TOTAL TIME: 15 min.

1-1/2	cups deli coleslaw
2	tablespoons stone-ground mustard
6	submarine buns, split
3/4	pound thinly sliced corned beef
12	dill pickle slices
12	slices Swiss cheese, halved

In a small bowl, combine coleslaw and mustard. Spread about 2 tablespoons over each bun half. Top with corned beef, pickles and cheese. Place on a baking sheet. Broil 4-6 in. from the heat for 3 minutes or until cheese is melted.

Yield: 6 servings.

Nutritional Analysis: 2 sandwich halves equals 783 calories, 34 g fat (17 g saturated fat), 106 mg cholesterol, 2,002 mg sodium, 77 g carbohydrate, 5 g fiber, 38 g protein.

Speedy Side Dishes

While you're at the deli to pick up the fixings for Reuben Slaw Sandwiches, stop by the produce department for a container of cut-up fresh fruit. Or grab a bag of your family's favorite potato chips.

Substitution Secret

Vlasic Sandwich Stackers® work great for this recipe. If you can't find them at your store, just make slices from your jar of pickles at home.

Barbecued Beef Quesadillas

PREP/TOTAL TIME: 20 min.

1/2　cup sour cream
1/3　cup minced fresh cilantro
　1　teaspoon lime juice
　1　carton (18 ounces) fully cooked barbecued shredded beef
　8　flour tortillas (8 inches)
1/2　cup refried beans
　1　cup (4 ounces) shredded Mexican cheese blend
1-1/2　cups shredded lettuce
Chopped fresh tomatoes, optional

In a small bowl, combine the sour cream, cilantro and lime juice; set aside. Heat barbecued beef according to package directions. Spread four tortillas with refried beans; top each with 1/2 cup beef and 1/4 cup cheese. Top with remaining tortillas.

In a large skillet coated with nonstick cooking spray, heat quesadillas over medium heat for 1-2 minutes on each side or until lightly browned. Cut each into four wedges. Serve with shredded lettuce, sour cream sauce and tomatoes if desired.

Yield: 4 servings.

Nutritional Analysis: 4 wedges equals 726 calories, 25 g fat (12 g saturated fat), 84 mg cholesterol, 1,728 mg sodium, 87 g carbohydrate, 3 g fiber, 35 g protein.

Substitution Secret

You can substitute refrigerated shredded barbecued chicken for the beef in this recipe with equally delicious results.

Time-Saving Tip

Looking for a way to speed up this already-fast recipe? Get out your nonstick skillet and cook all four tortillas at one time!

Skillet Beef and Potatoes

PREP/TOTAL TIME: 25 min.

   3   medium potatoes, halved and cut into 1/4-inch slices
   1/3   cup water
   1/2   teaspoon salt
   1   pound boneless beef sirloin steak, cut into thin strips
   2   teaspoons garlic pepper blend
   1/2   cup chopped onion
   3   tablespoons olive oil, *divided*
   1-1/2   teaspoons minced fresh rosemary

Place potatoes, water and salt in a microwave-safe dish. Cover and microwave on high for 6-10 minutes or until tender; drain.

Season beef with pepper blend. In a large skillet, stir-fry beef and onion in 2 tablespoons oil for 5 minutes or until beef is no longer pink. Meanwhile, in another skillet, stir-fry potatoes in remaining oil for 5 minutes or until browned. Stir in beef mixture. Sprinkle with rosemary.

Yield: 4 servings.

Nutritional Analysis: 1-1/2 cups equals 320 calories, 16 g fat (4 g saturated fat), 63 mg cholesterol, 487 mg sodium, 20 g carbohydrate, 2 g fiber, 23 g protein.

Don't Peel Potatoes

To decrease prep time (and increase nutrition), don't peel the potatoes.

Also, if you can, cook the potatoes ahead of time and refrigerate until ready to use.

Speedy Side Dish

Round out this hearty meat-and-potatoes meal with a side salad. Your grocery store likely carries a savory assortment of salad kits, which include the salad greens, dressing and other condiments all in one bag.

Reuben Chowder

PREP/TOTAL TIME: 25 min.

1	small onion, sliced
1	tablespoon vegetable oil
2	cans (14-1/2 ounces *each*) vegetable broth
1	can (14-1/2 ounces) beef broth
2	teaspoons prepared horseradish
1	teaspoon Worcestershire sauce
1/2	teaspoon ground mustard
1/4	teaspoon celery salt
5	ounces deli corned beef, chopped
1	cup sauerkraut, rinsed and well drained
2	slices rye bread, cubed
4	slices Swiss cheese

In a small skillet, saute onion in oil until tender. Meanwhile, in a large saucepan, bring the vegetable and beef broth to a boil; stir in the horseradish, Worcestershire sauce, mustard and celery salt. Add the corned beef, sauerkraut and onion. Reduce heat to low; cover and simmer for 10 minutes.

Ladle soup into four ovenproof bowls; top with bread cubes and Swiss cheese. Broil 3-4 in. from the heat for 2-3 minutes or until cheese is melted.

Yield: 4 servings.

Nutritional Analysis: 1-1/2 cups equals 263 calories, 15 g fat (7 g saturated fat), 50 mg cholesterol, 2,207 mg sodium, 15 g carbohydrate, 2 g fiber, 18 g protein.

Corned Beef History

According to the USDA, corned beef and cabbage was a traditional Easter Sunday dinner in Ireland.

During the winter, the beef was preserved. It was then enjoyed after the long, meatless Lenten fast.

Substitution Secret

This dish contains all of your favorite Reuben sandwich ingredients in a delicious soup. If you don't have rye bread, simply cut the Swiss cheese into strips and place it on the broth.

Quick & Easy **Beef**

Curried Beef Sandwiches

PREP/TOTAL TIME: 10 min.

1/3	cup mayonnaise
1/4	cup chutney
1/4	teaspoon curry powder
12	slices whole wheat bread
1-1/4	pounds thinly sliced deli roast beef
6	lettuce leaves
6	tomato slices

In a small bowl, combine the mayonnaise, chutney and curry. Spread about 1 tablespoon over six slices of bread; top with beef, lettuce, tomato and remaining bread.

Yield: 6 sandwiches.

Nutritional Analysis: 1 sandwich equals 360 calories, 15 g fat (3 g saturated fat), 29 mg cholesterol, 1,241 mg sodium, 36 g carbohydrate, 5 g fiber, 23 g protein.

Eat Your Veggies!

Keep carrot and celery sticks on hand for a fast side dish. Clean and slice carrots and celery as soon as you come home from the store. Place in a covered container and refrigerate in the crisper for up to 2 weeks.

Substitution Secret

For a little variety, substitute the roast beef with deli turkey, ham or a combination of all three meats. You can also offer white, rye, whole grain or sourdough bread along with the whole wheat.

Beef Veggie Casserole

PREP/TOTAL TIME: 25 min.

> 1 envelope mushroom gravy mix
> 3/4 cup water
> 2 cups cubed cooked beef
> 2 cups frozen mixed vegetables
> 2 medium potatoes, peeled, cubed and cooked
> 1 tube (12 ounces) refrigerated buttermilk biscuits, separated into 10 biscuits

In a large saucepan, combine gravy mix and water until smooth. Bring to a boil; cook and stir for 1 minute or until thickened. Stir in the beef, vegetables and potatoes; heat through.

Transfer to a greased 8-in. square baking dish. Top with biscuits. Bake, uncovered, at 400° for 12-16 minutes or until bubbly and biscuits are golden brown.

Yield: 5 servings.

Nutritional Analysis: 1 cup beef mixture with 2 biscuits equals 467 calories, 14 g fat (5 g saturated fat), 56 mg cholesterol, 1,010 mg sodium, 61 g carbohydrate, 4 g fiber, 25 g protein.

Preparation Pointer

For Sunday dinner, prepare your favorite roast beef and baked potatoes. Save 2 cups beef and 2 baked potatoes for this satisfying casserole on Monday night.

Serve a Side Salad

With lots of meat, hearty chunks of potato and plenty of mixed vegetables, Beef Veggie Casserole makes a wonderful meal with a green salad.

Asian Flank Steak Stir-Fry

PREP/TOTAL TIME: 25 min.

  4 ounces uncooked Asian rice noodles
  2 teaspoons cornstarch
  3 tablespoons soy sauce
  2 tablespoons rice wine vinegar
  2 tablespoons hoisin sauce
  1 teaspoon minced gingerroot
  1 teaspoon minced garlic
 1/4 teaspoon salt
 1/4 teaspoon pepper
  1 package (16 ounces) frozen stir-fry vegetable blend
1-1/2 cups shredded carrots
  2 teaspoons sesame oil, *divided*
1-1/2 pounds beef flank steak, cut into thin strips
  2 teaspoons sesame seeds, toasted

In a large bowl, soak noodles in boiling water for 10 minutes. Meanwhile, in a small bowl, combine the cornstarch, soy sauce, vinegar, hoisin sauce, ginger, garlic, salt and pepper until blended; set aside.

In a large skillet or wok, stir-fry the vegetable blend and carrots in 1 teaspoon oil for 2-3 minutes or until crisp-tender. Remove and keep warm. In the same pan, stir-fry beef in remaining oil for 3-4 minutes or until no longer pink.

Stir soy sauce mixture and add to pan. Bring to a boil; cook and stir for 1-2 minutes or until thickened. Drain noodles. Stir noodles and vegetables into beef mixture; heat through. Sprinkle with sesame seeds.

Yield: 6 servings.

Nutritional Analysis: 1-1/3 cups equals 294 calories, 11 g fat (4 g saturated fat), 48 mg cholesterol, 757 mg sodium, 25 g carbohydrate, 4 g fiber, 23 g protein.

Rice Noodle Knowledge

Dried Asian rice noodles are made with rice flour and can be found in larger grocery stores. Before using, they must be soaked in boiling water until soft and transparent.

Rice Wine Vinegar

Made from fermented rice, rice wine vinegar has a mild flavor and is popular in Asian cooking. If you can't find rice wine vinegar in your grocery store, simply substitute 1 tablespoon cider vinegar and 1 tablespoon water.

Steaks with Chipotle Sauce

PREP: 10 min.   **GRILL:** 15 min.

  1 **can (7 ounces) chipotle peppers in adobo sauce**
1/2 **cup sour cream**
  1 **teaspoon dried cilantro flakes**
  4 **New York strip steaks (8 ounces *each*)**

Chop one chipotle pepper; place in a bowl. Add 1 teaspoon of the adobo sauce. Stir in sour cream and cilantro; refrigerate. (Save remaining peppers and sauce for another use.)

Grill steaks, uncovered, over medium-hot heat for 6-10 minutes on each side or until meat reaches desired doneness (for rare, a meat thermometer should read 140°; medium, 160°; well-done, 170°). Serve with chipotle sauce.

Editor's Note: When cutting or seeding hot peppers, use rubber or plastic gloves to protect your hands. Avoid touching your face.

Yield: 4 servings.

Nutritional Analysis: 1 steak with 2 tablespoons sauce equals 517 calories, 36 g fat (16 g saturated fat), 144 mg cholesterol, 174 mg sodium, 2 g carbohydrate, trace fiber, 41 g protein.

Grilled Veggie Packets

A few minutes before grilling the steaks, put on a foil packet of fresh veggies. Cut up some ears of fresh corn, red potatoes and zucchini; place on a large piece of foil. Drizzle with olive oil. Sprinkle with salt, onion powder, garlic powder and Italian seasoning. Fold foil around the vegetables and seal tightly. Grill for 20-25 minutes, turning once.

Note About Chipotle

Chipotles in adobo sauce are dried smoked red jalapeno peppers, which are canned with a thick chili puree called adobo. They can be found in the Mexican section of your local supermarket.

Beef Burgundy Baskets

PREP/TOTAL TIME: 30 min.

  1 package (10 ounces) frozen puff pastry shells
  2 cups whole fresh mushrooms, cut in half
  2 tablespoons vegetable oil
  1 jar (16 ounces) pearl onions, drained
  2 packages (17 ounces *each*) refrigerated beef tips with gravy
1/4 cup burgundy wine
  1 teaspoon dried thyme

Bake pastry shells according to package directions. In a large skillet, cook mushrooms in oil for 2-3 minutes or until browned. Add onions; cook for 1 minute. Add the beef tips with gravy, wine and thyme; heat through. Carefully remove top of pastry shells; fill with beef mixture.

Yield: 6 servings.

Nutritional Analysis: 1 cup equals 504 calories, 27 g fat (6 g saturated fat), 63 mg cholesterol, 1,012 mg sodium, 38 g carbohydrate, 5 g fiber, 28 g protein.

Speedy Side Dish

For a vegetable dish to serve with Beef Burgundy Baskets, make some asparagus. Trim 1 pound fresh asparagus and place in a saucepan. Add 1/2 in. water; bring to a boil. Reduce heat; cover and simmer for 3-5 minutes or until crisp-tender. Top with melted butter; season with salt and pepper.

Secret Substitution

Instead of cutting whole fresh mushrooms in half, buy an 8-ounce package of sliced mushrooms and reduce the cooking time.

Slow-Cooked Swiss Steak

PREP: 15 min.   **COOK:** 8 hours

- 3/4 cup all-purpose flour
- 1 teaspoon pepper
- 1/4 teaspoon salt
- 2 to 2-1/2 pounds boneless beef top round steak
- 1 to 2 tablespoons butter
- 1 can (10-3/4 ounces) condensed cream of mushroom soup, undiluted
- 1-1/3 cups water
- 1 cup sliced celery, optional
- 1/2 cup chopped onion
- 1 to 3 teaspoons beef bouillon granules
- 1/2 teaspoon minced garlic

In a shallow bowl, combine the flour, pepper and salt. Cut steak into six serving-size pieces; dredge in flour mixture.

In a large skillet, brown steak in butter. Transfer to a 3-qt. slow cooker. Combine the remaining ingredients; pour over steak. Cover and cook on low for 8-9 hours or until meat is tender.

Yield: 6 servings.

Nutritional Analysis: 1 steak with about 1/2 cup gravy equals 313 calories, 9 g fat (4 g saturated fat), 92 mg cholesterol, 666 mg sodium, 18 g carbohydrate, 2 g fiber, 37 g protein.

Lively Leftover

Double the recipe for Slow-Cooked Swiss Steak for speedy Stroganoff. Cut up the meat, add sour cream to the gravy and serve over egg noodles.

Mashed Potatoes in Minutes

Think you can't serve your family mashed potatoes on a busy weeknight? Think again! Head to your grocery store and pick up a poly-bag of refrigerated or frozen mashed potatoes.

Quicker Beef Potpie

PREP/TOTAL TIME: 30 min.

Pastry for single-crust pie (9 inches)
- 1   tablespoon water
- 1/3   cup shredded cheddar cheese
- 3/4   teaspoon dried thyme, *divided*
- 1   pound boneless beef sirloin steak *or* boneless beef top round steak, cut into thin strips
- 1   tablespoon vegetable oil
- 1   package (16 ounces) frozen mixed vegetables
- 1   jar (12 ounces) beef gravy
- 1   can (4 ounces) mushroom stems and pieces, drained
- 1/2   teaspoon garlic salt
- 1/8   teaspoon pepper

On a floured surface, roll pastry to 1/8-in. thickness. Brush with water. Sprinkle with cheese and 1/4 teaspoon thyme; press lightly. Using a 3-in. biscuit cutter, cut out four 3-in. circles. Place circles and remaining pastry on ungreased baking sheets. Bake at 450° for 8-10 minutes or until golden brown.

In a large skillet over medium-high heat, brown beef in oil for 5 minutes or until no longer pink; drain. Stir in the vegetables, gravy, mushrooms, garlic salt, pepper and remaining thyme; bring to a boil. Reduce heat; cover and simmer for 15 minutes or until vegetables are tender.

Set pastry circles aside. Break remaining pastry into 2-in. pieces; place in soup bowls. Top with beef mixture and pastry circles.

Yield: 4 servings.

Nutritional Analysis: 1 serving equals 536 calories, 27 g fat (11 g saturated fat), 90 mg cholesterol, 1,120 mg sodium, 45 g carbohydrate, 6 g fiber, 31 g protein.

Preparation Pointer

After you purchase the beef for this recipe, slice it into thin strips right away. Place in a heavy-duty resealable plastic bag and freeze in a single layer. The meat will thaw much faster this way.

Time-Saving Tip

When you anticipate a busy day, prepare the cheese-topped pastry for Quicker Beef Potpie the night before. When cool, transfer to an airtight container and refrigerate until ready to use.

Thai Beef Salad

PREP/TOTAL TIME: 20 min.

  7 tablespoons olive oil, *divided*
  2 tablespoons lime juice, *divided*
  2 tablespoons chili sauce
1/2 teaspoon dried cilantro flakes
  6 cups shredded napa *or* Chinese cabbage
  2 cups shredded carrots
  1 cup chopped seeded peeled cucumber
1-1/2 pounds boneless beef sirloin steak, cut into thin strips
  2 teaspoons minced garlic
  1 teaspoon ground coriander
  1 teaspoon dried basil

In a jar with a tight-fitting lid, combine 6 tablespoons oil, 1 tablespoon lime juice, chili sauce and cilantro; shake well. In a large bowl, combine the cabbage, carrots and cucumber. Drizzle with dressing and toss to coat; arrange on four plates.

In a large skillet, cook the beef, garlic, coriander and basil in remaining oil for 5-6 minutes or until meat is no longer pink. Sprinkle with remaining lime juice. Spoon beef and pan juices over salad.

Yield: 4 servings.

Nutritional Analysis: 1 cup beef mixture with 1-1/4 cups salad equals 488 calories, 32 g fat (7 g saturated fat), 94 mg cholesterol, 221 mg sodium, 13 g carbohydrate, 4 g fiber, 35 g protein.

Napa Cabbage Knowledge

Napa cabbage, also known as Chinese cabbage, has white ribs and green leaves. It's commonly used in Asian cooking and can be found year-round in the produce section of your local grocery store.

Substitution Secret

When you're pressed for time, one package (16 ounces) coleslaw mix can be substituted for the napa cabbage, carrots and cucumber.

Busy cooks can depend on chicken when they want to offer their family a flavorful variety of entrees throughout the year.

Chicken
Cordon Bleu (p. 82)

Cookin' with Chicken

Monday Chicken Supper

PREP: 15 min.　**COOK:** 6 hours

> 4　medium carrots, cut into 2-inch pieces
> 1　medium onion, chopped
> 1　celery rib, cut into 2-inch pieces
> 2　cups cut fresh green beans (2-inch pieces)
> 5　small red potatoes, quartered
> 1　broiler/fryer chicken (3 to 3-1/2 pounds), cut up
> 4　bacon strips, cooked and crumbled
> 1-1/2　cups hot water
> 2　teaspoons chicken bouillon granules
> 1　teaspoon salt
> 1/2　teaspoon dried thyme
> 1/2　teaspoon dried basil

Pinch pepper

In a 5-qt. slow cooker, layer the first seven ingredients in order listed. In a bowl, combine the water, bouillon, salt, thyme, basil and pepper; pour over the top. Do not stir.

Cover and cook on low for 6-7 hours or until vegetables are tender and chicken juices run clear. Remove chicken and vegetables. Thicken cooking juices for gravy if desired.

Yield: 4 servings.

Nutritional Analysis: 1 serving equals 510 calories, 25 g fat (7 g saturated fat), 137 mg cholesterol, 1,262 mg sodium, 24 g carbohydrate, 6 g fiber, 47 g protein.

Lively Leftover

An opened package of sliced bacon should be refrigerated and used within 1 week. Use the leftover bacon from Monday Chicken Supper to make a bacon-and-egg breakfast on Saturday morning.

Thickening Juices

To thicken the juices in the slow cooker after the meat and vegetables are tender, combine 1 tablespoon of cornstarch with 1/4 cup cold water. Slowly pour into the slow cooker; stir until mixed well. Cover and cook on low for 30 minutes.

Garden Chicken Panini

PREP/TOTAL TIME: 20 min.

  2 packages (12 ounces *each*) refrigerated breaded
     chicken breast tenders
1/4 cup butter, softened
  8 slices Italian bread
1/4 cup tomato sauce
1/4 cup giardiniera
  8 slices mozzarella cheese

Heat chicken tenders in the microwave according to package directions. Butter one side of each slice of bread. Place four slices,
buttered side down, on a griddle or panini grill. Spread each
slice with 1 tablespoon tomato sauce; top with two to three chick-
en tenders, 1 tablespoon giardiniera and two slices of cheese. Top
with remaining bread, butter side up. Cook over medium heat until golden brown, turning once if using a griddle.

Yield: 4 servings.

Nutritional Analysis: 1 sandwich equals 653 calories, 33 g fat (17 g saturated fat),
145 mg cholesterol, 1,567 mg sodium, 49 g carbohydrate, 3 g fiber, 41 g protein.

Guide to Giardiniera

Giardiniera, a pickled vegetable mixture, is avail-
able in mild and hot varieties and can be found in
the Italian or pickle section
of your grocery store.

Soup and Sandwich Supper

While the paninis are cooking, open a can of condensed
tomato soup and prepare as
directed for a satisfying
soup and sandwich dinner.

Cookin' with **Chicken**

Chicken Bread Salad

PREP: 15 min. + chilling

24 slices French bread (3/4 inch thick)
3 cups cubed cooked chicken breast
4 medium tomatoes, cut into chunks
1 can (15-1/2 ounces) great northern beans, rinsed and drained
1 large cucumber, seeded and chopped
1/4 cup chopped fresh basil
1/4 teaspoon salt
1/4 teaspoon pepper
3/4 cup balsamic vinaigrette
1/2 cup shredded Parmesan cheese

Place bread on a baking sheet. Broil 3-4 in. from the heat for 2-3 minutes or until golden brown, turning once. Cool on a wire rack. Cut bread into 1-in. pieces.

In a large bowl, combine the bread, chicken, tomatoes, beans, cucumber, basil, salt and pepper. Drizzle with vinaigrette and toss to coat. Refrigerate for 30 minutes. Sprinkle with Parmesan cheese and toss.

Yield: 6 servings.

Nutritional Analysis: 1-3/4 cups equals 981 calories, 17 g fat (4 g saturated fat), 59 mg cholesterol, 2,245 mg sodium, 154 g carbohydrate, 13 g fiber, 50 g protein.

A Lesson in Melon

Because Chicken Bread Salad has plenty of vegetables and bread, all you need to round out the meal is honeydew melon. Purchase melons that are firm with a bit of softness at the stem end. They should feel heavy for their size.

Seeding a Cucumber

Here's a simple way to seed a cucumber. Cut it in half lengthwise. Scoop out the seeds with a teaspoon and discard.

Chicken Satay Wraps

PREP/TOTAL TIME: 15 min.

> 2 **tablespoons olive oil**
> 2 **tablespoons creamy peanut butter**
> 2 **green onions, chopped**
> 1 **teaspoon reduced-sodium soy sauce**
> 1/4 **teaspoon pepper**
> 2 **cups sliced cooked chicken**
> 1 **cup coleslaw mix**
> 4 **flour tortillas (8 inches), warmed**

In a large bowl, whisk the oil, peanut butter, onions, soy sauce and pepper until combined. Add the chicken and toss to coat. Sprinkle 1/4 cup coleslaw mix over each tortilla; top with chicken mixture. Roll up tightly.

Yield: 4 servings.

Nutritional Analysis: 1 wrap equals 321 calories, 16 g fat (3 g saturated fat), 62 mg cholesterol, 325 mg sodium, 23 g carbohydrate, 3 g fiber, 26 g protein.

Time-Saving Tip

Refrigerated grilled chicken strips can be used to speed up the preparation of this already-simple recipe.

Try Other Tortillas

For a change from traditional flour tortillas, try whole wheat, spinach or sun-dried tomato.

Cookin' with **Chicken**

Garlic Chicken 'n' Gravy

PREP/TOTAL TIME: 25 min.

- 4 boneless skinless chicken breast halves (4 ounces *each*)
- 1/4 teaspoon salt
- 1/4 teaspoon pepper
- 5 garlic cloves, peeled and chopped
- 2 tablespoons butter
- 1/2 cup plus 2 tablespoons chicken broth, *divided*
- 1/2 cup white wine
- 1/2 teaspoon dried basil
- 1/4 teaspoon dried oregano
- 1 tablespoon all-purpose flour

Sprinkle chicken with salt and pepper. In a large skillet, cook chicken and garlic in butter over medium-high heat for 5 minutes or until browned. Add 1/2 cup broth, wine, basil and oregano. Bring to a boil. Reduce heat; cover and simmer for 7-9 minutes or until chicken is no longer pink.

Remove chicken with a slotted spoon and keep warm. In a small bowl, combine flour and remaining broth until smooth; stir into pan juices. Bring to a boil; cook and stir for 1-2 minutes or until thickened. Serve over chicken.

Yield: 4 servings.

Nutritional Analysis: 1 chicken breast half with 3 tablespoons gravy equals 208 calories, 8 g fat (4 g saturated fat), 78 mg cholesterol, 407 mg sodium, 3 g carbohydrate, trace fiber, 24 g protein.

Peeling and Chopping Fresh Garlic

To quickly peel garlic cloves, place on a cutting board. With the flat side of a chef's knife, press down until you hear the peel crack; remove and discard peel. Coarsely chop the garlic.

Speedy Side Dish

Mashed potatoes and cooked carrots nicely complement this meaty entree. Prepare refrigerated mashed potatoes as the package directs. Then turn to page 287 for an awesome Cider-Glazed Carrots recipe!

Cider-Glazed Carrots (p. 287)

Chicken Cordon Bleu

PREP/TOTAL TIME: 30 min.

    4 boneless skinless chicken breast halves
    2 teaspoons Dijon mustard
 1/2 teaspoon paprika
    4 thin slices fully cooked ham
    1 cup soft bread crumbs
 1/4 cup grated Parmesan cheese
 1/4 teaspoon pepper
    3 to 4 tablespoons mayonnaise

SAUCE:

    1 tablespoon butter
    1 tablespoon all-purpose flour
    1 cup milk
 1/4 teaspoon salt
 1/2 cup shredded Swiss cheese
    2 tablespoons white wine

Flatten the chicken to 1/2-in. thickness. Spread mustard on one side; sprinkle with paprika. Top each with a ham slice. Roll up tightly; secure with toothpicks. In a bowl, combine bread crumbs, Parmesan cheese and pepper. Brush chicken with mayonnaise; roll in crumb mixture. Place in a shallow 2-qt. microwave-safe dish; cover loosely. Microwave on high for 5-1/2 minutes; turn chicken. Cook 7 minutes more or until juices run clear; keep warm.

In a 1-qt. microwave-safe dish, heat butter on high for 20 seconds; stir in flour until smooth. Cook, uncovered, on high for 20 seconds. Add milk and salt. Cook 2-3 minutes longer or until thickened. Stir in cheese until smooth. Add wine. Discard toothpicks from chicken; top with sauce.

Editor's Note: This recipe was tested in a 1,1000-watt microwave.

Yield: 4 servings.

Nutritional Analysis: 1 serving equals 470 calories, 24 g fat (9 g saturated fat), 140 mg cholesterol, 840 mg sodium, 12 g carbohydrate, trace fiber, 49 g protein.

Preparation Pointer

Soft bread crumbs are made from fresh bread. To make your own, tear fresh white, French or whole wheat bread into 1-in. pieces. Place in a food processor or blender. Cover and push the pulse button several times to make coarse crumbs.

Two slices of bread yield 1 cup of crumbs.

Time-Saving Tip

To flatten chicken breasts in a flash (and with little mess!), put them in a resealable plastic bag and seal. Pound the chicken with the flat side of a meat mallet.

Chinese Chicken Soup

PREP/TOTAL TIME: 25 min.

- **3** cans (14-1/2 ounces *each*) chicken broth
- **1** package (16 ounces) frozen stir-fry vegetable blend
- **2** cups cubed cooked chicken
- **1** teaspoon minced fresh gingerroot
- **1** teaspoon soy sauce
- **1/4** teaspoon sesame oil

In a large saucepan, combine all ingredients. Bring to a boil. Reduce heat; cover and simmer for 15 minutes or until heated through.

Yield: 6 servings.

Nutritional Analysis: 1-1/2 cups equals 149 calories, 4 g fat (1 g saturated fat), 42 mg cholesterol, 936 mg sodium, 11 g carbohydrate, 3 g fiber, 17 g protein.

Easy Accompaniment

Instead of a typical sandwich, offer a platter of egg rolls with steaming bowls of Chinese Chicken Soup. Your grocer likely offers both refrigerated and frozen varieties.

Fun Dessert Idea

Continue with the Oriental theme by serving fortune cookies for dessert. Look for a box in the Asian cooking aisle of your supermarket.

Apple Chicken Slaw

PREP/TOTAL TIME: 10 min.

1/4   cup poppy seed salad dressing
5   teaspoons mayonnaise
2   cups cubed cooked chicken breast
2   cups coleslaw mix
1   medium apple, chopped
Lettuce leaves, optional

In a small bowl, combine salad dressing and mayonnaise. In a large bowl, combine the chicken, coleslaw mix and apple. Drizzle with dressing and toss to coat. Serve on lettuce-lined plates if desired.

Yield: 4 servings.

Nutritional Analysis: 1 cup equals 266 calories, 14 g fat (2 g saturated fat), 67 mg cholesterol, 193 mg sodium, 11 g carbohydrate, 2 g fiber, 22 g protein.

Preparation Pointer

When a recipe calls for cooked chicken and you don't have any leftovers, stop by your grocer's deli and pick up a rotisserie chicken. One chicken usually yields 2 to 3 cups chopped meat.

Salad Stir-Ins

Jazz up the flavor of Apple Chicken Slaw by tossing in some slivered almonds, canned mandarin oranges or seedless grapes.

Cookin' with **Chicken**

Saucy Apricot Chicken

PREP/TOTAL TIME: 25 min.

> 4 boneless skinless chicken breast halves (4 ounces *each*)
> 1/4 teaspoon salt
> 1/4 teaspoon pepper
> 2 tablespoons butter
> 1 can (15 ounces) apricot halves
> 3 teaspoons cornstarch
> 1/4 cup apricot preserves
> 2 tablespoons white wine vinegar
> 4 green onions, chopped

Hot cooked rice, optional

Sprinkle chicken with salt and pepper. In a large skillet, cook chicken in butter over medium heat for 5 minutes, turning occasionally. Cover and cook 5 minutes longer or until juices run clear. Remove and keep warm.

Drain apricots, reserving juice. Cut apricots into 1/2-in. slices; set aside. In a small bowl, combine cornstarch and reserved juice until smooth. Stir in preserves and vinegar until combined; pour into skillet. Bring to a boil over medium heat; cook and stir for 1-2 minutes or until thickened. Add apricots and chicken; heat through. Sprinkle with onions. Serve with rice if desired.

Yield: 4 servings.

Nutritional Analysis: 1 chicken breast half with 1/2 cup sauce (calculated without rice) equals 324 calories, 8 g fat (4 g saturated fat), 78 mg cholesterol, 275 mg sodium, 39 g carbohydrate, 2 g fiber, 24 g protein.

Speedy Side Dish

Instead of ordinary white rice, prepare a package of instant brown rice, which cooks in about 10 minutes. For terrific flavor, use chicken broth for the liquid called for in the recipe.

Substitution Secret

Canned peach or pear halves can be used in place of the apricot halves if your family prefers. The apricot preserves would still pair well with those fruits.

Tortellini Chicken Salad

PREP: 20 min. + chilling

2   packages (9 ounces *each*) refrigerated tricolor cheese tortellini
4   cups cubed cooked chicken breast
1   can (6 ounces) pitted ripe olives, drained and halved
2   medium tomatoes, chopped
1   cup cubed part-skim mozzarella cheese
1/3   cup minced fresh parsley
3/4   teaspoon salt
3/4   teaspoon pepper
3/4   cup balsamic vinaigrette
1/2   cup shredded Parmesan cheese

Cook tortellini according to package directions; drain and rinse in cold water. In a large bowl, combine the tortellini, chicken, olives, tomatoes, mozzarella cheese, parsley, salt and pepper. Drizzle with vinaigrette and toss to coat. Cover and refrigerate for at least 4 hours. Just before serving, sprinkle with Parmesan cheese and toss.

Yield: 8 servings.

Nutritional Analysis: 1-1/2 cups equals 396 calories, 17 g fat (5 g saturated fat), 82 mg cholesterol, 1,024 mg sodium, 27 g carbohydrate, 3 g fiber, 35 g protein.

Preparation Pointer

Tortellini Chicken Salad needs time to chill, making it a perfect entree to prepare either the night before or earlier in the day.

Substitution Secret

There are many types of cheese tortellini on the market. Substitute any kind you like if you can't find the tricolor variety.

Spicy Chicken Stew

PREP/TOTAL TIME: 30 min.

> 3 pounds boneless skinless chicken thighs, cut into 1/2-inch pieces
> 2 teaspoons minced garlic
> 2 tablespoons olive oil
> 1 can (15 ounces) garbanzo beans *or* chickpeas, rinsed and drained
> 1 can (14-1/2 ounces) diced tomatoes with onions, undrained
> 1 cup lime-garlic salsa
> 1 teaspoon ground cumin
> 1/3 cup minced fresh cilantro
>
> Sour cream, optional

In a Dutch oven, cook chicken and garlic in oil for 5 minutes. Stir in the beans, tomatoes, salsa and cumin. Cover and simmer for 15 minutes or until chicken is no longer pink. Stir in cilantro. Garnish with sour cream if desired.

Yield: 6 servings.

Nutritional Analysis: 1-1/2 cups equals 344 calories, 16 g fat (3 g saturated fat), 92 mg cholesterol, 645 mg sodium, 19 g carbohydrate, 3 g fiber, 29 g protein.

Preparation Pointer

You can purchase boneless skinless chicken thighs in your grocer's meat department. If you can't find them, just ask!

Time-Saving Tip

Although Spicy Chicken Stew takes just half an hour from start to finish, consider preparing it the night before and reheating the next day for a meal in mere minutes.

Mango Chicken Curry

PREP/TOTAL TIME: 30 min.

1/2	cup chopped onion
1	medium sweet red pepper, julienned
2	teaspoons vegetable oil
1-1/2	pounds boneless skinless chicken breasts, cut into thin strips
1	tablespoon curry powder
2	teaspoons minced fresh gingerroot
1	teaspoon minced garlic
1/2	teaspoon salt
1/8	teaspoon cayenne pepper
1	cup chopped peeled mango
3/4	cup coconut milk
2	tablespoons tomato paste

Hot cooked rice, optional

Go with Mango!

Slice up any remaining mango and use it to garnish individual plates.

Coconut Milk Clues

Coconut milk can be found in the Asian section of your grocery store. Don't confuse coconut milk with cream of coconut, which is a thick, sweet liquid often used in making alcoholic beverages.

In a large skillet, saute onion and red pepper in oil for 2-4 minutes or until crisp-tender. Add the chicken, curry, ginger, garlic, salt and cayenne. Cook and stir for 5 minutes. Stir in the mango, coconut milk and tomato paste; bring to a boil. Reduce heat; cover and simmer for 10 minutes or until chicken is no longer pink. Serve with rice if desired.

Yield: 4 servings.

Nutritional Analysis: 1-1/4 cups chicken mixture (calculated without rice) equals 343 calories, 16 g fat (9 g saturated fat), 94 mg cholesterol, 392 mg sodium, 15 g carbohydrate, 3 g fiber, 36 g protein.

Cookin' with **Chicken**

Sweet Potato Chicken Stew

PREP: 15 min.   **COOK:** 25 min.

3	cups cubed peeled sweet potatoes
1/2	cup water
1-1/2	pounds boneless skinless chicken breasts, cut into 1/2-inch cubes
2	tablespoons vegetable oil
3	cups shredded cabbage
3	cups chicken broth
1	can (15-1/2 ounces) black-eyed peas, rinsed and drained
1	can (14-1/2 ounces) diced tomatoes with onions, undrained
1	cup sliced celery
1	cup tomato juice
1	teaspoon pepper
1/2	teaspoon salt

Place the sweet potatoes and water in a 2-qt. microwave-safe dish. Cover and microwave on high for 6 minutes or until tender; drain.

In a Dutch oven, saute the chicken in oil for 8-9 minutes or until no longer pink. Add the cabbage, broth, peas, tomatoes, celery, tomato juice, pepper, salt and sweet potatoes. Bring to a boil. Reduce heat; cover and simmer for 20 minutes or until heated through.

Editor's Note: This recipe was tested in a 1,100-watt microwave.

Yield: 8 servings.

Nutritional Analysis: 1-1/2 cups equals 250 calories, 6 g fat (1 g saturated fat), 47 mg cholesterol, 907 mg sodium, 27 g carbohydrate, 4 g fiber, 22 g protein.

Lively Leftover

Refrigerate leftover cabbage in a resealable plastic bag for up to 7 days and use to make Brown Rice Veggie Stir-Fry (page 200), Thai Beef Salad (page 70) or Pineapple Cabbage Saute (page 262).

Secret to Shredding Cabbage

To easily shred cabbage, first cut a head of cabbage into quarters. Finely slice each quarter so that thin strands fall away.

Guacamole Chicken Roll-Ups

PREP/TOTAL TIME: 15 min.

> 1/4 **cup guacamole**
> 4 **flavored flour tortillas of your choice (10 inches)**
> 4 **large lettuce leaves**
> 1-1/3 **cups chopped fresh tomatoes**
> 2 **packages (6 ounces *each*) thinly sliced deli smoked chicken breast**
> 2 **cups (8 ounces) shredded Mexican cheese blend**

Spread 1 tablespoon of guacamole over each tortilla. Layer with lettuce, tomatoes, chicken and cheese. Roll up tightly.

Yield: 4 servings.

Nutritional Analysis: 1 roll-up equals 523 calories, 26 g fat (13 g saturated fat), 89 mg cholesterol, 1,428 mg sodium, 41 g carbohydrate, 3 g fiber, 34 g protein.

Serve Soup On the Side

In a saucepan, saute 1 medium chopped onion and 2 minced garlic cloves in 1 tablespoon vegetable oil for 2-3 minutes or until tender.

In a blender or food processor, place 1/2 cup chicken broth and 1 can (15 ounces) rinsed and drained black beans; cover and process until smooth. Add to onion mixture.

Stir in 1 undrained can (10 ounces) diced tomatoes and green chilies, 1 teaspoon ground cumin, 1/2 teaspoon garlic salt and 1-1/2 cups chicken broth. Drain and rinse 2 cans (15 ounces *each*) black beans and add to the soup. Bring to a boil. Reduce heat; cover and simmer for 10 minutes.

Cookin' with **Chicken**

Nutty Chicken Fettuccine

PREP/TOTAL TIME: 30 min.

1/4	cup all-purpose flour
2	tablespoons ground walnuts
1	teaspoon curry powder
1/4	teaspoon salt
1/4	teaspoon ground cinnamon
1/4	teaspoon pepper
1-1/2	pounds boneless skinless chicken breasts, cut into thin strips
1	medium sweet red pepper, julienned
1/4	cup chopped onion
3	tablespoons olive oil
8	ounces uncooked fettuccine
1	cup milk
1	package (8 ounces) cream cheese, cubed
1/2	cup shredded Parmesan cheese
1/3	cup chopped walnuts, toasted

In a large resealable plastic bag, combine the first six ingredients. Add chicken in batches; toss to coat. In a large skillet, saute the chicken, red pepper and onion in oil for 6-8 minutes until chicken juices run clear and vegetables are crisp-tender.

Meanwhile, cook fettuccine according to package directions. In a saucepan, combine the milk, cream cheese and Parmesan cheese; cook and stir over medium heat for 5 minutes or until cheese is melted and sauce is smooth. Drain fettuccine; top with chicken mixture and sauce. Sprinkle with toasted walnuts.

Yield: 4 servings.

Nutritional Analysis: 1 serving equals 772 calories, 47 g fat (19 g saturated fat), 172 mg cholesterol, 452 mg sodium, 36 g carbohydrate, 3 g fiber, 52 g protein.

Substitution Secrets

Use any color of bell pepper or pasta in this recipe. You can also stir in some sliced fresh mushrooms or frozen peas.

Toasted Nut Know-How

Toasting nuts intensifies their flavor and adds crunch. You can toast nuts in a skillet over medium heat, stirring frequently. Or place in a single layer in a shallow baking pan and bake at 350° for 10 to 15 minutes, stirring often.

Gnocchi Chicken Skillet

PREP/TOTAL TIME: 25 min.

   1   **package (10 ounces) potato gnocchi**
   1   **pound ground chicken**
 1/2 **cup chopped onion**
   2   **tablespoons olive oil**
   1   **jar (26 ounces) spaghetti sauce**
 1/4 **to 1/2 teaspoon dried oregano**
 1/4 **teaspoon salt**
Shredded Parmesan cheese, optional

Prepare gnocchi according to package directions. Meanwhile, in a large skillet, cook chicken and onion in oil over medium heat until chicken is no longer pink. Stir in spaghetti sauce, oregano and salt. Drain gnocchi; add to skillet. Cover and cook for 10-15 minutes or until heated through. Serve with Parmesan cheese if desired.

Yield: 4 servings.

Nutritional Analysis: 1-1/2 cups equals 512 calories, 24 g fat (5 g saturated fat), 85 mg cholesterol, 1,445 mg sodium, 49 g carbohydrate, 5 g fiber, 27 g protein.

Choose Ground Chicken!

Ground chicken is a great substitute in recipes calling for ground beef because it reduces the fat but not the flavor.

Fresh ground chicken should be refrigerated and used within 2 days. For longer storage, freeze for up to 3 months.

Chicken Chili

PREP: 10 min.   **COOK:** 5 hours

1-1/2 pounds boneless skinless chicken breasts, cut into 1/2-inch cubes
1 cup chopped onion
3 tablespoons vegetable oil
1 can (15 ounces) cannellini *or* white kidney beans, rinsed and drained
1 can (14-1/2 ounces) diced tomatoes, undrained
1 can (14-1/2 ounces) diced tomatoes with mild green chilies, undrained
1 cup frozen corn
1 teaspoon salt
1 teaspoon ground cumin
1 teaspoon minced garlic
1/2 teaspoon celery salt
1/2 teaspoon ground coriander
1/2 teaspoon pepper
Sour cream and shredded cheddar cheese, optional

In a large skillet, saute chicken and onion in oil for 5 minutes or until chicken is browned. Transfer to a 5-qt. slow cooker. Stir in the beans, tomatoes, corn and seasonings. Cover and cook on low for 5 hours or until chicken is no longer pink. Garnish with sour cream and cheese if desired.

Yield: 6 servings.

Nutritional Analysis: 1 cup equals 318 calories, 10 g fat (2 g saturated fat), 63 mg cholesterol, 1,092 mg sodium, 28 g carbohydrate, 6 g fiber, 28 g protein.

Serving Suggestions

Just before serving Chicken Chili, cook some elbow macaroni and offer it as another topping. To give the chili even more Southwestern flavor, garnish individual servings with minced fresh cilantro.

Speedy Side Dish

You can rely on a variety of refrigerated breads to round out meals featuring chili, stew and soups. Keep tubes of biscuits, crescent rolls, corn bread twists, crusty French loaf and dinner rolls on hand.

Chicken Breast Cacciatore

PREP/TOTAL TIME: 30 min.

>   1   can (8 ounces) tomato sauce
>   1   teaspoon Italian seasoning
>   1/4   teaspoon garlic powder
>   1/2   cup crushed cornflakes
>   1/4   cup grated Parmesan cheese
>   1   teaspoon dried parsley flakes
>   1   egg
>   6   boneless skinless chicken breast halves (4 ounces *each*)
>   2/3   cup shredded mozzarella cheese

In a microwave-safe bowl, combine the tomato sauce, Italian seasoning and garlic powder. Cover and microwave on high for 1-1/2 minutes; stir. Cook at 50% power for 2-4 minutes or until mixture simmers, stirring once; set aside.

In a shallow bowl, combine the cornflakes, Parmesan cheese and parsley. In another shallow bowl, beat the egg. Dip chicken into egg, then roll in cornflake mixture. Place in a lightly greased shallow 3-qt. microwave-safe dish.

Cover and microwave on high for 8 to 9-1/2 minutes, rotating a half turn after 4 minutes. Pour tomato mixture over chicken; sprinkle with mozzarella cheese. Cook, uncovered, at 50% power for 2-4 minutes or until chicken juices run clear.

Editor's Note: This recipe was tested in a 1,100-watt microwave.

Yield: 6 servings.

Nutritional Analysis: 1 serving equals 241 calories, 8 g fat (3 g saturated fat), 121 mg cholesterol, 410 mg sodium, 9 g carbohydrate, trace fiber, 33 g protein.

Speedy Side Dish

Use your microwave to make corn on the cob to serve alongside Chicken Breast Cacciatore.

Place 4 husked ears of corn in a shallow microwave-safe dish. Add 1/4 cup water. Cover and microwave on high for 10-13 minutes, turning once. Let stand for 5 minutes; drain. Brush with melted butter; sprinkle with salt and Parmesan cheese. (This recipe was tested in an 850-watt microwave.)

Time-Saving Tip

Keep a box of cornflake crumbs in your cupboard for a quick chicken coating. You'll find boxes of crushed cornflakes in your supermarket by the bread crumbs.

Quicker Chicken 'n' Dumplings

PREP/TOTAL TIME: 30 min.

    4 cups chicken broth
1/2 cup sliced celery
1/2 cup sliced carrots
    1 bay leaf
1-1/2 teaspoons dried parsley flakes, *divided*
    2 cups biscuit/baking mix
1/4 teaspoon dried thyme
Dash ground nutmeg
2/3 cup milk
    3 cups cubed cooked chicken breast

In a 5-qt. Dutch oven or kettle, combine the broth, celery, carrots, bay leaf and 1 teaspoon parsley; bring to a boil.

For dumplings, combine the biscuit mix, thyme and nutmeg in a bowl; stir in milk and remaining parsley just until moistened. Drop by tablespoonfuls onto boiling broth. Cook, uncovered, for 10 minutes; cover and cook 10 minutes longer.

With a slotted spoon, remove dumplings to a serving dish; keep warm. Bring broth to a boil; reduce heat. Add chicken; heat through. Discard bay leaf. Spoon over dumplings.

Yield: 4 servings.

Nutritional Analysis: 1 cup equals 374 calories, 9 g fat (0 saturated fat), 69 mg cholesterol, 858 mg sodium, 48 g carbohydrate, 0 fiber, 26 g protein.

Preparation Pointer

To accurately measure the biscuit/baking mix, spoon into a standard dry-ingredient measuring cup, then level the top with a straight-edge utensil. Do not scoop it or pack it down.

Time-Saving Tip

Keep cans of ready-to-serve chicken broth in your pantry to give recipes a head start.

One 14-1/2 ounce can of ready-to-serve chicken broth equals 1-3/4 cups.

Spinach-Feta Stuffed Chicken

PREP: 15 min.   **COOK:** 20 min.

6	boneless skinless chicken breast halves (4 ounces *each*)
1/2	cup frozen chopped spinach, thawed and squeezed dry
5	ounces crumbled feta cheese, *divided*
3	tablespoons all-purpose flour
1	teaspoon dried oregano
1/2	teaspoon salt
1/2	teaspoon pepper
1	tablespoon olive oil
2	cans (14-1/2 ounces *each*) diced tomatoes with onions, undrained

Hot cooked pasta, optional

Flatten chicken to 1/4-in. thickness. Combine spinach and 1/2 cup feta cheese; spoon down the center of each chicken breast half. Fold chicken over filling and secure with toothpicks. Combine the flour, oregano, salt and pepper; rub over chicken.

In a large skillet, brown chicken in oil on all sides. Discard toothpicks. Place chicken in a greased shallow 3-qt. microwave-safe dish. Top with tomatoes and remaining feta cheese. Cover and microwave on high for 18-20 minutes or until chicken juices run clear and cheese is melted. Serve over pasta if desired.

Editor's Note: This recipe was tested in a 1,100-watt microwave.

Yield: 6 servings.

Nutritional Analysis: 1 serving (calculated without pasta) equals 267 calories, 9 g fat (4 g saturated fat), 75 mg cholesterol, 834 mg sodium, 15 g carbohydrate, 3 g fiber, 29 g protein.

Microwave Cooking Tip

Once the stuffed chicken breasts are browned in a skillet, cooking them in the microwave gets them done quickly. Be sure to check each piece of chicken—particularly those in the center of the baking dish—to be sure they are thoroughly cooked.

Carrot Chicken Pilaf

PREP: 20 min.   **COOK:** 20 min. + standing

1 pound boneless skinless chicken breasts, cut into thin strips
1/4 cup butter
1-1/2 cups uncooked long grain rice
5 medium carrots, sliced
1 medium onion, chopped
1/2 cup sliced fresh mushrooms
1/4 cup chopped sweet red pepper
4 cups chicken broth
2 tablespoons minced fresh parsley

Storing Rice

Rice is a super staple to have on hand because it cooks quickly and rounds out many mouth-watering meals. Store an open container of uncooked white rice in an airtight container in a cool, dark place for up to 2 years. Brown rice should be used within 6 months.

In a large skillet, brown chicken in butter. Remove and keep warm. Add the rice, carrots, onion, mushrooms and red pepper to the skillet. Cook and stir until rice is browned and onion is tender.

Stir in broth. Place chicken over rice mixture. Bring to a boil. Reduce heat; cover and simmer for 20-25 minutes or until rice is tender. Stir in parsley. Let stand for 5 minutes before serving.

Yield: 6 servings.

Nutritional Analysis: 1 cup equals 362 calories, 10 g fat (5 g saturated fat), 62 mg cholesterol, 755 mg sodium, 46 g carbohydrate, 3 g fiber, 21 g protein.

Blue Cheese Chicken Pitas

PREP/TOTAL TIME: 10 min.

1 package (10 ounces) ready-to-use grilled Italian chicken strips
1 cup shredded carrots
1 cup shredded romaine
1 large tomato, seeded and chopped
1/4 cup real bacon bits
1/2 cup blue cheese salad dressing
2 whole wheat pita breads (6 inches), halved

In a bowl, combine the first five ingredients. Add dressing and toss to coat. Stuff each pita half with 1/2 cup chicken salad.

Yield: 2 servings.

Nutritional Analysis: 2 filled pita halves equals 734 calories, 39 g fat (8 g saturated fat), 100 mg cholesterol, 1,489 mg sodium, 59 g carbohydrate, 8 g fiber, 46 g protein.

Preparation Pointer

When feeding a few more people, it's easy to double the recipe for Blue Cheese Chicken Pitas.

Substitution Secrets

If your family doesn't favor blue cheese salad dressing, replace it with another creamy variety, such as ranch, peppercorn or Parmesan.

The chicken salad mixture can also be served on regular bread or rolls and on lettuce leaves. Or stir in some cooked elbow macaroni for a hearty lunch.

Barbecued Chicken Bake

PREP/TOTAL TIME: 30 min.

  1 **carton (32 ounces) refrigerated shredded barbecued chicken**
  1 **can (15-1/2 ounces) hominy, rinsed and drained**
1/4 **cup canned chopped green chilies**
  1 **package (11-1/2 ounces) refrigerated corn bread twists**

In a large bowl, combine the chicken, hominy and chilies. Pour into an 11-in. x 7-in. x 2-in. baking dish coated with nonstick cooking spray.

Separate corn bread twists into strips. Place four strips diagonally in each direction over chicken mixture, forming a lattice crust. Press ends against sides of baking dish. Bake at 375° for 20-25 minutes or until crust is golden brown.

Yield: 6 servings.

Nutritional Analysis: 3/4 cup equals 316 calories, 8 g fat (2 g saturated fat), 0 cholesterol, 785 mg sodium, 32 g carbohydrate, 2 g fiber, 5 g protein.

Hints About Hominy

Hominy is hulled corn kernels that have been stripped of their bran and germ. (When ground, hominy is called grits.) The kernels look somewhat like popcorn and have a soft, chewy consistency. Look for hominy in the canned vegetables aisle.

Preparation Pointer

You can find ready-to-heat barbecued chicken in the refrigerated meat section of your local grocery store. Then just add three ingredients and you have a tasty casserole!

Ground Chicken Gumbo

PREP/TOTAL TIME: 30 min.

 1 cup uncooked long grain rice
 1 pound ground chicken
 1 cup chopped celery
 1 cup chopped green pepper
 1/2 cup chopped onion
 2 tablespoons olive oil
 1 can (28 ounces) crushed tomatoes
 1 cup sliced fresh okra
 1 cup chicken broth
 1 teaspoon Cajun seasoning
 1 teaspoon salt
 1 teaspoon dried oregano
 1 teaspoon ground thyme
 1/4 teaspoon hot pepper sauce

Cook rice according to package directions. Meanwhile, in a Dutch oven, cook the chicken, celery, green pepper and onion in oil over medium heat for 8 minutes or until chicken is no longer pink; drain.

Stir in the remaining ingredients. Bring to a boil. Reduce heat; cover and simmer for 20 minutes or until heated through. Serve over rice.

Yield: 6 servings.

Nutritional Analysis: 1 cup gumbo with 1/2 cup rice equals 322 calories, 11 g fat (2 g saturated fat), 50 mg cholesterol, 900 mg sodium, 40 g carbohydrate, 5 g fiber, 18 g protein.

Know Your Okra

Purchase fresh okra that is firm, brightly colored and less than 4 inches long. Refrigerate unwashed okra in a plastic bag for up to 3 days. Before cooking, wash and trim ends. One pound equals 2 cups chopped.

If you can't find fresh okra, look for packages of sliced okra in the freezer section.

Baked Mushroom Chicken

PREP/TOTAL TIME: 30 min.

> 4 cups sliced fresh mushrooms
> 3 tablespoons butter, *divided*
> 6 boneless skinless chicken breast halves (4 ounces each)
> 1/4 teaspoon salt
> 1/4 teaspoon pepper
> 1/2 cup chicken broth
> 1/4 cup sherry

In a large skillet, saute the mushrooms in 2 tablespoons butter until tender. Place the chicken in a greased shallow 3-qt. baking dish; sprinkle with salt and pepper. Melt remaining butter; drizzle over chicken. Combine the broth and sherry; pour over chicken. Spoon mushrooms over top. Cover and bake at 400° for 20-25 minutes or until chicken is no longer pink.

Yield: 6 servings.

Nutritional Analysis: 1 serving equals 192 calories, 9 g fat (4 g saturated fat), 78 mg cholesterol, 291 mg sodium, 2 g carbohydrate, 1 g fiber, 24 g protein.

Equivalents for Mushrooms

An 8-ounce package of sliced mushrooms equals about 2-1/2 cups. One pound whole fresh mushrooms yields about 5 cups sliced.

Speedy Side Dish

Round out this chicken dinner with your family's favorite cooked vegetables and a long grain and wild rice mix.

Sesame Chicken and Noodles

PREP/TOTAL TIME: 30 min.

8 ounces thin spaghetti
2 tablespoons sesame oil, *divided*
1 tablespoon cornstarch
1 cup chicken broth
1/4 cup soy sauce
1 tablespoon rice wine vinegar
1-1/2 pounds boneless skinless chicken breasts, cut into 1/2-inch cubes
1 package (8 ounces) sliced baby portobello mushrooms
1 medium sweet red pepper, chopped
1 teaspoon minced garlic
1 package (9 ounces) fresh baby spinach
1/2 cup chopped green onions
3 tablespoons sherry
2 teaspoons minced fresh gingerroot
1 tablespoon sesame seeds, toasted

Cook spaghetti according to package directions; drain. Toss with 1 tablespoon sesame oil; set aside. In a small bowl, combine the cornstarch, broth, soy sauce and vinegar until smooth; set aside.

In a large skillet, stir-fry chicken, mushrooms, red pepper and garlic in remaining oil for 5-8 minutes or until chicken is browned. Stir broth mixture and add to the skillet. Bring to a boil; cook and stir for 2 minutes or until thickened and chicken is no longer pink. Add spinach; cover and cook for 2-3 minutes or until spinach is wilted. Add the onions, sherry, ginger and spaghetti; cook for 2-3 minutes or until heated through. Sprinkle with sesame seeds.

Yield: 6 servings.

Nutritional Analysis: 1-1/4 cups equals 358 calories, 9 g fat (2 g saturated fat), 63 mg cholesterol, 871 mg sodium, 36 g carbohydrate, 3 g fiber, 32 g protein.

Storing and Thawing Chicken

Refrigerate fresh raw chicken in its original unopened wrapper and use within 1 or 2 days.

For longer storage, wrap individual meal-size portions of chicken in plastic wrap, then place in a freezer bag. Whole chickens can be frozen for 1 year, but chicken parts should be used within 9 months. Never refreeze thawed chicken.

Always be sure to cook or freeze raw chicken by the "use by" date.

Boneless skinless chicken breasts will thaw in the refrigerator overnight. Bone-in chicken parts and whole chickens may take 1 to 2 days longer.

Once thawed, chicken can be kept in the refrigerator 1 to 2 days longer. Never thaw chicken at room temperature, even if frozen inside. The surface of foods can warm up quickly, allowing bacteria to grow.

Basil Cream Chicken

PREP/TOTAL TIME: 25 min.

1/4 cup milk

1/4 cup dry bread crumbs

4 boneless skinless chicken breast halves (4 ounces *each*)

3 tablespoons butter

1/2 cup chicken broth

1 cup heavy whipping cream

1 jar (4 ounces) sliced pimientos, drained

1/2 cup grated Parmesan cheese

1/4 cup minced fresh basil

1/8 teaspoon pepper

Place milk and bread crumbs in separate shallow bowls. Dip chicken in milk, then coat with crumbs. In a skillet over medium-high heat, cook chicken in butter on both sides until juices run clear, about 10 minutes. Remove and keep warm.

Add broth to the skillet. Bring to a boil over medium heat; stir to loosen browned bits. Stir in the cream and pimientos; boil and stir for 1 minute. Reduce heat. Add Parmesan cheese, basil and pepper; cook and stir until heated through. Pour over the chicken.

Yield: 4 servings.

Nutritional Analysis: 1 chicken breast half with 1/3 cup sauce equals 493 calories, 37 g fat (22 g saturated fat), 177 mg cholesterol, 536 mg sodium, 9 g carbohydrate, 1 g fiber, 30 g protein.

Preparation Pointer

If you have time, let the crumb-coated chicken refrigerate for 1 hour before browning. The coating will cling to the chicken better when browning.

The Basics of Basil

The peppery, almost licorice-like flavor of basil enhances a wide range of foods and is a favorite seasoning around the world.

A few of the most common varieties of this aromatic herb are sweet basil, dwarf basil, Italian or curly basil, purple basil and lemon basil.

To store fresh basil, wrap it in barely damp paper towels, then in a plastic bag for up to 4 days. To keep for a week, place basil stems in a glass of water, cover with a plastic bag and refrigerate. Be sure to change the water daily.

Patties with Red Pepper Sauce

PREP/TOTAL TIME: 25 min.

1   **cup uncooked orzo pasta**
1   **cup frozen peas**
1   **package (10 ounces) refrigerated breaded chicken patties**
1   **jar (12 ounces) roasted sweet red peppers, drained**
1   **teaspoon chipotle peppers in adobo sauce**
1/3 **cup shredded mozzarella cheese**

Prepare orzo and peas according to package directions. Meanwhile, place chicken patties in a 13-in. x 9-in. x 2-in. baking dish coated with nonstick cooking spray. Bake, uncovered, at 425° for 10-12 minutes or until heated through.

In a blender, cover and process red and chipotle peppers until pureed; transfer to a microwave-safe bowl. Cover and microwave on high for 1 minute. Spoon over chicken patties; sprinkle with cheese. Bake 5 minutes longer or until cheese is melted. Drain orzo and peas; combine. Serve with chicken.

Yield: 4 servings.

Nutritional Analysis: 1 chicken patty with 3 tablespoons sauce and 3/4 cup orzo mixture equals 470 calories, 15 g fat (5 g saturated fat), 50 mg cholesterol, 634 mg sodium, 62 g carbohydrate, 3 g fiber, 22 g protein.

Speedy Side Dish

Pasta is a perfect partner for Patties with Red Pepper Sauce.

Prepare 4 ounces uncooked angel hair pasta according to package directions, adding 1 peeled and halved garlic clove to the water. Drain; discard garlic.

Place pasta in a serving bowl; add 2 tablespoons butter. Toss gently until butter melts. Add 2 tablespoons Parmesan cheese, 1/2 teaspoon minced fresh parsley and 1/4 teaspoon garlic salt. Toss to coat.

Cookin' with **Chicken**

Pear Walnut Chicken

PREP/TOTAL TIME: 25 min.

1   can (15-1/4 ounces) sliced pears
1/2 cup unsweetened apple juice
1/4 cup packed brown sugar
3   tablespoons soy sauce
1/2 teaspoon garlic powder
1-1/2 pounds boneless skinless chicken
      breasts, cut into 1-inch cubes
3   tablespoons vegetable oil
2   tablespoons minced fresh
      parsley
2   tablespoons cornstarch
1/4 cup cold water
1/2 cup chopped walnuts
Hot cooked rice, optional

Drain pears, reserving juice in a 1-cup measuring cup. Add enough water to measure 3/4 cup. Set pears aside. In a small bowl, combine the pear juice mixture, apple juice, brown sugar, soy sauce and garlic powder; set aside.

In a large skillet, saute chicken in oil for 4-6 minutes or until no longer pink. Add parsley and pear juice mixture. Cover and simmer for 5-7 minutes, stirring occasionally.

In a small bowl, combine cornstarch and cold water until smooth; pour into skillet. Bring to a boil; cook and stir for 1 minute or until thickened. Stir in walnuts and pears. Serve over rice if desired.

Yield: 6 servings.

Nutritional Analysis: 1 cup chicken mixture (calculated without rice) equals 348 calories, 16 g fat (2 g saturated fat), 63 mg cholesterol, 66 mg sodium, 27 g carbohydrate, 1 g fiber, 26 g protein.

Rice Variety Yields

Not sure how much rice will feed your family? Plan on 1/2 cup rice per person.

Here are some easy equivalents:

One cup instant rice equals 2 cups cooked.

One cup converted rice equals about 3-1/2 cups cooked.

One cup brown rice equals 4 cups cooked.

Grilled Jerk Chicken

PREP: 10 min. + marinating   **GRILL:** 30 min.

- **4 teaspoons curry powder**
- **4 teaspoons ground cumin**
- **4 teaspoons paprika**
- **3 teaspoons ground ginger**
- **3 teaspoons ground allspice**
- **1 teaspoon salt**
- **1 teaspoon cayenne pepper**
- **1 teaspoon coarsely ground pepper**
- **4 bone-in chicken breast halves with skin (8 ounces each)**
- **4 chicken thighs with skin (4 ounces each)**

In a small bowl, combine the first eight ingredients; rub over chicken pieces. Cover and refrigerate for 1 hour. Grill the chicken, covered, over indirect medium heat for 30-40 minutes or until juices run clear.

Yield: 4 servings.

Nutritional Analysis: 1 chicken breast half and 1 thigh equals 444 calories, 21 g fat (6 g saturated fat), 167 mg cholesterol, 741 mg sodium, 6 g carbohydrate, 3 g fiber, 56 g protein.

Just What Is "Jerk"?

"Jerk" refers to a dry seasoning blend that originated on a Caribbean island. The ingredients can vary but usually includes peppers (like cayenne or chilies) and spices (like allspice, ginger and cinnamon).

Sweet Side Dish

Grilled Asparagus (page 259) and Cherry Tomato Corn Salad (page 283) pair wonderfully with Grilled Jerk Chicken.

But for a tasty side dish that's a bit sweet, try grilling bananas! Keeping the peel on, cut firm bananas in half horizontally. Spray the cut side with butter-flavored cooking spray. Grill for 1 minute on each side. Brush the cut side with molasses and serve.

Grilled Asparagus (p. 259)

Cherry Tomato Corn Salad (p. 283)

From down-home dinners to more elegant entrees, turkey solves any dining dilemma.

Turkey Pizza (p. 144)

Timeless Turkey

Turkey Breast with Mushroom Sauce

PREP: 10 min.   **COOK:** 7 hours

- 1 boneless turkey breast (3 pounds), halved
- 2 tablespoons butter, melted
- 2 tablespoons dried parsley flakes
- 1/2 teaspoon dried tarragon
- 1/2 teaspoon salt
- 1/8 teaspoon pepper
- 1 jar (4-1/2 ounces) sliced mushrooms, drained
- 1/2 cup white wine
- 2 tablespoons cornstarch
- 1/4 cup cold water

Place the turkey, skin side up, in a 5-qt. slow cooker. Brush with butter. Sprinkle with parsley, tarragon, salt and pepper. Top with mushrooms. Pour wine over all. Cover and cook on low for 7-8 hours.

Remove turkey and keep warm. Skim fat from cooking juices. In a small saucepan, combine cornstarch and water until smooth. Gradually add cooking juices. Bring to a boil; cook and stir for 2 minutes or until thickened. Serve with turkey.

Yield: 8 servings.

Nutritional Analysis: 5 ounces cooked turkey with 3 tablespoons sauce equals 245 calories, 10 g fat (2 g saturated fat), 106 mg cholesterol, 945 mg sodium, 3 g carbohydrate, trace fiber, 34 g protein.

Cook It Quicker

For even faster preparation, slow cook Turkey Breast with Mushroom Sauce on high for 3 to 4 hours. Continue with the recipe as directed.

Speedy Side Dish

Oven-Roasted Potatoes wonderfully round out any meal. Cut 2 pounds small unpeeled red potatoes into wedges; place in a 13-in. x 9-in. x 2-in. baking pan. Drizzle with 2 tablespoons olive oil. Sprinkle with 1 teaspoon crushed dried rosemary, 1/2 teaspoon salt and 1/4 teaspoon pepper; toss to coat.

Bake at 450° for 20-30 minutes or until potatoes are golden brown and tender.

Artichoke Turkey Salami Salad

PREP: 20 min. + chilling

4   cups cooked elbow macaroni
2   cups (8 ounces) shredded mozzarella cheese
2   cups cherry tomatoes, halved
8   ounces turkey salami, cut into thin strips
1   cup roasted sweet red peppers, drained and cut into strips
1   can (7-1/2 ounces) marinated artichoke hearts, drained and chopped
1   can (2-1/4 ounces) sliced ripe olives, drained
1/3   cup Italian salad dressing
1/4   cup minced fresh basil
1/2   teaspoon pepper

In a large salad bowl, combine the macaroni, mozzarella, tomatoes, salami, red peppers, artichokes and olives. Add dressing, basil and pepper; toss to coat. Cover and refrigerate for 2 hours or overnight. Toss before serving.

Yield: 8 servings.

Nutritional Analysis: 1-1/4 cups equals 303 calories, 18 g fat (6 g saturated fat), 44 mg cholesterol, 754 mg sodium, 23 g carbohydrate, 2 g fiber, 13 g protein.

Preparation Pointer

One 7-ounce package of uncooked elbow macaroni yields about 4 cups cooked.

Try Turkey Salami

Turkey salami is a sausage made from ground dark turkey meat, flavored with garlic and other seasonings. It's coarse and dry in texture. Turkey salami contains approximately 50 percent less fat than regular salami.

Caribbean Turkey Burgers

PREP/TOTAL TIME: 20 min.

1/2   cup dry bread crumbs
3   tablespoons chopped green onions
3   tablespoons minced fresh parsley
2   tablespoons Worcestershire sauce
1   tablespoon Caribbean jerk seasoning
1/2   teaspoon salt
1-1/4   pounds lean ground turkey
1   teaspoon olive oil
4   whole wheat hamburger buns, split
4   lettuce leaves
1   medium mango, peeled and sliced
4   sweet red pepper rings

Time-Saving Tip

When you come home from the grocery store with fresh ground turkey, assemble these Caribbean Turkey Burgers right away.

Then freeze in a single layer in a resealable plastic freezer bag.

To use, thaw overnight in the refrigerator and cook as directed.

In a large bowl, combine the first six ingredients. Crumble turkey over the mixture and mix just until combined. Shape into four 1/2-in.-thick patties.

In a large skillet, cook patties in oil over medium heat for 5 minutes on each side or until no longer pink. Serve on buns with lettuce, mango slices and red pepper rings.

Yield: 4 servings.

Nutritional Analysis: 1 burger equals 436 calories, 16 g fat (4 g saturated fat), 112 mg cholesterol, 1,048 mg sodium, 44 g carbohydrate, 5 g fiber, 31 g protein.

Turkey Pear Skillet

PREP: 10 min.   **COOK:** 25 min.

2 **tablespoons cornstarch**
1 **cup chicken broth**
1/2 **cup sweet white wine**
1/2 **cup cranberry juice**
1 **teaspoon rubbed sage**
1/4 **teaspoon salt**
1 **package (20 ounces) turkey breast tenderloins, cut into thin strips**
1 **cup thinly sliced onion**
2 **tablespoons olive oil**
3 **medium pears, peeled and sliced**
1/2 **cup chopped walnuts**
1/2 **cup dried cranberries**
2 **tablespoons minced fresh parsley**
Hot cooked long grain and wild rice mix, optional

In a small bowl, combine the cornstarch, broth, wine, cranberry juice, sage and salt until blended; set aside. In a large skillet, saute turkey and onion in oil for 10-12 minutes or until meat is no longer pink.

Stir broth mixture and add to skillet. Bring to a boil; cook and stir for 2 minutes or until thickened. Add the pears, walnuts, cranberries and parsley; cover and cook for 3 minutes or until heated through. Serve with rice if desired.

Yield: 6 servings.

Nutritional Analysis: 1 cup turkey mixture (calculated without rice) equals 328 calories, 12 g fat (1 g saturated fat), 46 mg cholesterol, 307 mg sodium, 30 g carbohydrate, 3 g fiber, 25 g protein.

Basic Brussels Sprouts

To boil whole brussels sprouts, remove any yellow outer leaves and trim ends. Cut an "X" in the core end with a sharp knife. Add 1 in. water to a saucepan; add brussels sprouts. Bring to a boil.

Reduce heat; cover and simmer for 10 to 12 minutes or until crisp-tender. Drain. Top with melted butter. Four cups of brussels sprouts feeds 4 to 6 people.

Substitution Secret

Turkey breast slices or chicken breasts—cut into thin strips—can be substituted for tenderloin strips.

Ground Turkey and Hominy

PREP/TOTAL TIME: 20 min.

1-1/2 pounds ground turkey
1 large onion, chopped
1 teaspoon minced garlic
2 tablespoons olive oil
2 cans (14-1/2 ounces *each*) diced tomatoes, undrained
1 tablespoon chili powder
1-1/2 teaspoons ground cumin
1 teaspoon salt
1/2 teaspoon ground mustard
1/2 teaspoon dried thyme
1/4 teaspoon ground cinnamon
1/4 teaspoon ground allspice
1/4 teaspoon pepper
2 cans (15-1/2 ounces *each*) hominy, rinsed and drained

Speedy Side Dish

Green beans pair well with hearty Ground Turkey and Hominy. Place a 16-ounce package of frozen French-style green beans in a saucepan. Cover with water; cook until crisp-tender.

In a skillet over low heat, toast 1/2 cup slivered almonds in 1/4 cup butter. Remove from the heat; stir in 2 teaspoons lemon juice and 1/4 teaspoon salt. Drain beans. Add almond mixture and toss to coat.

In a large skillet, cook the turkey, onion and garlic in oil over medium heat until meat is no longer pink; drain. Stir in the tomatoes and seasonings; heat through. Add hominy and heat through.

Yield: 8 servings.

Nutritional Analysis: 1 cup equals 287 calories, 16 g fat (4 g saturated fat), 58 mg cholesterol, 989 mg sodium, 20 g carbohydrate, 5 g fiber, 16 g protein.

Saucy Turkey

PREP/TOTAL TIME: 30 min.

- 1/2 cup chopped green pepper
- 1/3 cup chopped onion
- 2 tablespoons butter
- 1-1/2 cups ketchup
- 1/2 cup chicken broth
- 1-1/2 teaspoons Worcestershire sauce
- 1 teaspoon prepared mustard
- 1/4 to 1/2 teaspoon hot pepper sauce
- 1/4 teaspoon pepper
- 3 cups cubed cooked turkey
- 4 sandwich buns, split, optional

In a large saucepan, saute the green pepper and onion in butter until tender. Stir in the ketchup, broth, Worcestershire sauce, mustard, hot pepper sauce and pepper. Add turkey. Simmer, uncovered, for 20 minutes or until heated through. Serve on buns if desired.

Yield: 4 servings.

Nutritional Analysis: 1-1/4 cups turkey mixture (calculated without bun) equals 338 calories, 11 g fat (5 g saturated fat), 95 mg cholesterol, 1,353 mg sodium, 28 g carbohydrate, 2 g fiber, 33 g protein.

Preparation Pointer

Purchase packages of both frozen chopped onions and green peppers. They are loose-packed so you can easily measure only as much as needed.

Save Some Turkey

If you plan on cooking a turkey breast over the weekend, pick up an extra one and add it to the oven! Set aside 3 cups cubed cooked turkey for this recipe.

Chutney Turkey Salad

PREP: 15 min. + chilling

3 cups cubed cooked turkey breast
1 cup chopped celery
1 cup golden raisins
4 ounces Monterey Jack cheese, cut into 1/2-inch cubes
3 tablespoons chopped green onions
1/3 cup mayonnaise
1/4 cup mango chutney
1/2 teaspoon ground ginger
1/4 teaspoon pepper
Lettuce leaves, optional

In a large bowl, combine the turkey, celery, raisins, cheese and onions. In a small bowl, combine the mayonnaise, chutney, ginger and pepper until blended. Pour over turkey mixture and toss to coat. Cover and refrigerate for 1 hour. Serve on a lettuce-lined plate if desired.

Yield: 4 servings.

Nutritional Analysis: 1 cup equals 567 calories, 25 g fat (7 g saturated fat), 127 mg cholesterol, 520 mg sodium, 46 g carbohydrate, 11 g fiber, 39 g protein.

Preparation Pointer

Chutney is a slightly spicy condiment containing fruit, vinegar, sugar and spices. The flavor can range from mild to hot. Look for it in the condiment or pickle aisle at your grocery store.

Speedy Side Dish

Bruschetta Polenta (page 264) is a colorful accompaniment to Chutney Turkey Salad. While the salad is chilling, you can quickly prepare the polenta.

Bruschetta Polenta (p. 264)

Swiss Turkey Tenderloin Strips

PREP/TOTAL TIME: 30 min.

  1   package (20 ounces) turkey breast tenderloins,
      cut into thin strips
1/2   teaspoon salt
1/4   teaspoon pepper
  3   tablespoons olive oil
  1   teaspoon minced garlic
  2   tablespoons all-purpose flour
  1   cup chicken broth
1/2   cup white wine
  3   cups (12 ounces) shredded Swiss cheese
  1   package (10 ounces) fresh spinach, trimmed
1/4   cup water

Cooking with White Wine

When cooking with wine, the alcohol is cooked off, leaving behind a fabulous flavor.

White wine for cooking should be strong and dry, not sour or fruity.

Wine labeled "cooking wine" has an inferior flavor. Instead, a good, dry white vermouth is an excellent choice to use.

Season turkey with salt and pepper. In a large skillet, saute turkey in oil for 6-8 minutes or until no longer pink. Remove with a slotted spoon and set aside.

In the drippings, saute garlic until tender. Stir in the flour, broth and wine until blended. Bring to a boil over medium heat; cook and stir for 1-2 minutes or until thickened. Reduce heat to low. Slowly add cheese; cook and stir for 2 minutes or until cheese is melted and sauce is blended.

Add turkey; heat through. Meanwhile, in a large saucepan or Dutch oven, cook spinach in water for 3-5 minutes or until wilted; drain. Serve turkey mixture over spinach.

Yield: 4 servings.

Nutritional Analysis: 1 cup equals 598 calories, 35 g fat (16 g saturated fat), 144 mg cholesterol, 872 mg sodium, 9 g carbohydrate, 2 g fiber, 59 g protein.

Turkey Stroganoff

PREP: 10 min.   **COOK:** 30 min.

- 1 package (20 ounces) turkey breast tenderloins, cut into 1/2-inch slices
- 2 tablespoons vegetable oil, *divided*
- 1 cup sliced fresh mushrooms
- 1 cup julienned sweet red pepper
- 1/2 cup chopped onion
- 3 tablespoons all-purpose flour
- 1/2 teaspoon salt
- 1/2 teaspoon dried thyme
- 1/4 teaspoon pepper
- 1 can (14-1/2 ounces) chicken broth
- 1 cup (8 ounces) sour cream
- 2 tablespoons Dijon mustard
- 2 tablespoons minced fresh parsley

Hot mashed potatoes, optional

In a large skillet, brown the turkey in 1 tablespoon oil over medium-high heat for 5 minutes, turning occasionally. Cover and cook for 5-8 minutes or until turkey is no longer pink; drain. Remove turkey and keep warm.

In the same skillet, saute the mushrooms, red pepper and onion in remaining oil for 3-5 minutes or until tender. Sprinkle with flour, salt, thyme and pepper. Stir in broth until blended. Bring to a boil; cook and stir for 1-2 minutes or until thickened.

Add the sour cream, mustard, parsley and turkey. Cook and stir for 3 minutes or until heated through. Serve with mashed potatoes if desired.

Yield: 4 servings.

Nutritional Analysis: 1-1/4 cups equals 380 calories, 19 g fat (8 g saturated fat), 107 mg cholesterol, 998 mg sodium, 12 g carbohydrate, 1 g fiber, 38 g protein.

Fresh Parsley Facts

Parsley is used to complement an assortment of foods. To store fresh parsley, wrap it in paper towels and place in a plastic bag; refrigerate. Or place the stems in a glass of water, cover the top with a plastic bag and refrigerate; change the water every few days.

Substitution Secret

You can also serve Turkey Stroganoff over hot cooked egg noodles.

Turkey Meatball Soup

PREP/TOTAL TIME: 30 min.

1 package (12 ounces) refrigerated fully cooked Italian turkey meatballs
1 can (49-1/2 ounces) chicken broth
2 cups uncooked egg noodles
2 cups cut fresh green beans
1 cup sliced fresh carrots
1 cup chopped celery
1 cup chopped onion
1 tablespoon dried parsley flakes
1 teaspoon garlic powder
1 teaspoon dried oregano
1 teaspoon dried basil
1/4 teaspoon pepper

In a Dutch oven, combine all ingredients. Bring to a boil. Reduce heat; simmer, uncovered, for 20-25 minutes or until noodles are tender.

Yield: 6 servings.

Nutritional Analysis: 1-1/3 cups equals 227 calories, 8 g fat (2 g saturated fat), 55 mg cholesterol, 1,357 mg sodium, 22 g carbohydrate, 4 g fiber, 17 g protein.

Fast Oven-Fresh Bread

While Turkey Meatball Soup is simmering, bake Red Onion Focaccia.

Slice 2 small red onions and separate into rings. In a large skillet, saute onions in 1 tablespoon olive oil for 4 minutes; set aside.

On a greased baking sheet, roll out one 10-ounce tube refrigerated pizza crust into a 12-in. x 8-in. rectangle. Brush with 2 tablespoons olive oil. Sprinkle with 4 tablespoons grated Romano cheese, 1 teaspoon crushed dried rosemary and 1 teaspoon garlic powder.

Bake at 425° for 14-16 minutes or until lightly browned.

Preparation Pointers

Cooked Italian turkey meatballs can be found in the refrigerated section of your local grocery store. You can also substitute frozen beef meatballs.

Turkey Bean Soup

PREP: 10 min.   **COOK:** 40 min.

1 **pound ground turkey**
1 **cup chopped onion**
1 **cup chopped celery**
1 **tablespoon olive oil**
1 **can (49-1/2 ounces) chicken broth**
2 **cups frozen corn**
1 **can (15 ounces) cannellini *or* white kidney beans, rinsed and drained**
1 **cup frozen lima beans**
1 **can (4 ounces) chopped green chilies**
1 **teaspoon dried oregano**
1 **teaspoon ground cumin**
1 **teaspoon chili powder**
1/2 **teaspoon salt**
Shredded cheddar cheese, optional

In a Dutch oven, cook the turkey, onion and celery in oil over medium heat until meat is no longer pink. Add the broth, corn, beans, chilies, oregano, cumin, chili powder and salt. Bring to a boil. Reduce heat; cover and simmer for 30 minutes or until heated through. Serve with cheese if desired.

Yield: 8 servings.

Nutritional Analysis: 1-1/2 cups equals 259 calories, 11 g fat (3 g saturated fat), 39 mg cholesterol, 1,052 mg sodium, 25 g carbohydrate, 6 g fiber, 16 g protein.

Speedy Side Dish

Serve Toasty Garlic Bread alongside steaming bowls of Turkey Bean Soup.

Cut a loaf of French bread into 1-in. slices. Spread both sides of each slice with softened butter.

Place cut side down on a baking sheet. Sprinkle with grated Parmesan cheese, dried parsley flakes and garlic powder.

Broil 4 in. from the heat until light golden brown. Turn slices and repeat.

136

Creamed Turkey on Mashed Potatoes

PREP/TOTAL TIME: 20 min.

1/2	cup chopped onion
2	tablespoons butter
2	tablespoons all-purpose flour
1/4	teaspoon salt
1/8	teaspoon white pepper
2	cups milk
2	cups cubed cooked turkey breast
1	cup frozen mixed vegetables
2	cups hot mashed potatoes

Preparation Pointers

Get a head start on this down-home dinner by stopping by the deli counter to pick up the mashed potatoes. While you're there, have them cut a thick slice of turkey breast, keeping in mind that 1 pound of turkey breast equals about 3 cups cubed.

In a large saucepan, saute the onion in butter until tender. Sprinkle with flour, salt and pepper. Stir in the milk until blended. Bring to a boil; cook and stir for 2 minutes or until thickened and bubbly. Add the turkey and vegetables; cover and simmer until heated through. Serve over mashed potatoes.

Yield: 4 servings.

Nutritional Analysis: 1 cup turkey mixture with 1/2 cup mashed potatoes equals 372 calories, 12 g fat (7 g saturated fat), 95 mg cholesterol, 594 mg sodium, 36 g carbohydrate, 2 g fiber, 30 g protein.

Pepperoni Penne Carbonara

PREP/TOTAL TIME: 30 min.

3 cups uncooked penne *or* medium tube pasta
2 cups chopped sun-dried tomatoes
(not packed in oil)
3 cups boiling water
1/2 teaspoon minced garlic
1/4 cup butter
1 cup sliced turkey pepperoni
1 cup shredded Parmesan cheese
1 cup heavy whipping cream
3 tablespoons minced fresh basil
1/2 teaspoon salt
1/4 teaspoon pepper

Cook pasta according to package directions. Meanwhile, in a large bowl, soak tomatoes in boiling water for 10 minutes; drain.

In a large skillet, saute the tomatoes and garlic in butter for 3 minutes. Stir in the pepperoni, Parmesan cheese, cream, basil, salt and pepper. Cook over low heat for 3 minutes or until heated through. Drain penne; toss with sauce.

Yield: 6 servings.

Nutritional Analysis: 1-1/2 cups equals 483 calories, 29 g fat (17 g saturated fat), 108 mg cholesterol, 1,245 mg sodium, 39 g carbohydrate, 4 g fiber, 19 g protein.

Chopping Sun-Dried Tomatoes

Sun-dried tomatoes can easily be cut into smaller pieces if you use a kitchen scissors.

Choosing the Perfect Pasta

Heavy sauces (like the one here) pair well with thick pasta shapes, such as penne, bow ties (farfalle), fettuccine, linguine and rigatoni.

Pasta shapes with holes or ridges, like mostaccioli or radiatore, are perfect for chunkier sauces.

Thin, delicate pastas, like angel hair or thin spaghetti, should be served with light, thin sauces.

Turkey Tenderloin Supreme

PREP/TOTAL TIME: 20 min.

1 package (20 ounces) turkey breast tenderloins, cut into 1-inch slices
1 tablespoon butter
1/3 cup chopped green onions
1 can (10-3/4 ounces) condensed cream of chicken soup, undiluted
1/4 cup water

In a large skillet, brown the turkey in butter. Add onions; cook for 1-2 minutes. Combine the soup and water; pour over turkey. Bring to a boil. Reduce heat; cover and simmer for 8-10 minutes or until meat juices run clear.

Yield: 4 servings.

Nutritional Analysis: 1 cup equals 245 calories, 9 g fat (4 g saturated fat), 83 mg cholesterol, 684 mg sodium, 6 g carbohydrate, 1 g fiber, 35 g protein.

Flavorful Rice

A side dish that combines vegetables and a starch is the perfect choice to serve with Turkey Tenderloin Supreme.

In a saucepan, combine 1 cup uncooked long grain rice, 2-1/4 cups water, 2 to 3 tablespoons onion soup mix and 1/4 teaspoon salt. Bring to a boil. Add 2 cups frozen mixed vegetables; return to a boil. Reduce heat; cover and simmer for 15 minutes. Cook until the rice and vegetables are tender.

Turkey with Balsamic-Honey Sauce

PREP/TOTAL TIME: 20 min.

1/2	cup balsamic vinegar
1/4	cup honey
4	teaspoons reduced-sodium soy sauce
2	eggs, lightly beaten
3/4	cup seasoned bread crumbs
1	package (17.6 ounces) turkey breast slices
2	tablespoons olive oil
1/4	cup raisins
1/4	cup slivered almonds

In a small bowl, whisk the vinegar, honey and soy sauce until blended; set aside. Place eggs and bread crumbs in separate shallow bowls. Dip turkey slices into eggs, then coat with crumbs.

In a large skillet, saute turkey in oil in batches for 2 minutes on each side or until no longer pink. Remove and keep warm. Stir vinegar mixture and add to the skillet; add the raisins and almonds. Cook and stir over medium heat for 5 minutes or until thickened. Serve over turkey.

Yield: 4 servings.

Nutritional Analysis: 2 turkey slices with 2 tablespoons sauce equals 471 calories, 15 g fat (2 g saturated fat), 184 mg cholesterol, 626 mg sodium, 46 g carbohydrate, 2 g fiber, 39 g protein.

Cooking with Vinegar

Vinegar loses much of its pungency when heated. If that's what you want, then add vinegar at the beginning of the cooking time.

However, if you want that jolt of acidity, stir in the vinegar toward the end of the cooking time or after the dish is removed from the heat.

Turkey Meat Loaf

PREP: 15 min.   **COOK:** 70 min. + standing

    1 cup chopped onion
    1 cup shredded carrots
  1/2 cup chopped celery
    1 tablespoon vegetable oil
1-1/2 cups crushed saltines (about 45 crackers)
  3/4 cup ketchup, *divided*
  1/4 cup minced fresh parsley
    1 egg, lightly beaten
    4 teaspoons ground mustard, *divided*
    2 teaspoons salt
    2 teaspoons minced garlic
    1 teaspoon pepper
2-1/2 pounds lean ground turkey
    2 tablespoons brown sugar

In a large skillet, saute the onion, carrots and celery in oil until tender. In a large bowl, combine the onion mixture, cracker crumbs, 1/2 cup ketchup, parsley, egg, 2 teaspoons mustard, salt, garlic and pepper. Crumble turkey over mixture and mix well.

Shape into a loaf. Place in a greased 13-in. x 9-in. x 2-in. baking dish. Bake, uncovered, at 350° for 1 hour.

In a small bowl, combine the brown sugar and remaining ketchup and mustard until smooth. Spoon over meat loaf. Bake 10-20 minutes longer or until meat is no longer pink and a meat thermometer reads 160°; drain. Let stand for 10 minutes before slicing.

Yield: 8 servings.

Nutritional Analysis: 2 slices equals 344 calories, 16 g fat (4 g saturated fat), 139 mg cholesterol, 1,158 mg sodium, 22 g carbohydrate, 2 g fiber, 28 g protein.

Blue Cheese Mashed Potatoes (p. 266)

Lively Leftover

Use leftover meat loaf to make special sandwiches for lunch the next day. Spread a zesty prepared mustard on slices of whole wheat, sourdough or white bread; top with a slice of cold meat loaf. Add a variety of toppings, such as lettuce, tomato, onion and pickles.

Speedy Side Dish

Offer your family a meat-and-potatoes meal they can't refuse by serving Blue Cheese Mashed Potatoes (page 266) alongside Turkey Meat Loaf.

Turkey Pizza

PREP: 15 min. **BAKE:** 25 min.

- 1 package (20 ounces) turkey Italian sausage links
- 1 teaspoon olive oil
- 2 tubes (10 ounces *each*) refrigerated pizza crust
- 1 can (15 ounces) pizza sauce
- 1 cup sliced red onion
- 1 can (14 ounces) water-packed artichoke hearts, rinsed, drained and chopped
- 2 large tomatoes, sliced
- 2 cups (8 ounces) shredded Italian-blend cheese

In a large skillet, cook sausage in oil over medium heat for 8-10 minutes or until no longer pink. Cut into 1/4-in. slices.

Press pizza dough into a greased 15-in. x 10-in. x 1-in. baking pan, building up edges slightly; seal seam. Prick dough thoroughly with a fork. Bake at 400° for 8 minutes or until lightly browned.

Spread with pizza sauce; top with sausage, onion, artichokes and tomatoes. Sprinkle with cheese. Bake for 15-20 minutes or until crust is golden brown.

Yield: 8 servings.

Nutritional Analysis: 2 pieces equals 433 calories, 16 g fat (6 g saturated fat), 56 mg cholesterol, 1,359 mg sodium, 46 g carbohydrate, 3 g fiber, 26 g protein.

Press Crust into The Pan

When patting the pizza crust into the pan, work from the center and use the tips of your fingertips to prevent tears in the crust.

Simple Salad Dressing

It's easy to encourage your family to dive into salads when you have a savory homemade dressing at the ready. Try this recipe to make 1/2 cup Italian salad dressing.

In a jar with a tight-fitting lid, combine 1/4 cup olive oil, 2 tablespoons red wine vinegar, 2 tablespoons water, 1/2 teaspoon sugar, 1/2 teaspoon Italian seasoning, 1/4 teaspoon salt and 1/4 teaspoon coarsely ground black pepper; shake well. Serve with salad greens and vegetables. Refrigerate leftovers.

Timeless **Turkey**

Guacamole Turkey BLTs

PREP/TOTAL TIME: 15 min.

12   slices ready-to-serve fully cooked bacon
3/4   cup guacamole
12   slices whole wheat bread, toasted
6   large lettuce leaves
12   slices tomato
1   pound thinly sliced deli turkey

Heat bacon according to package directions. Spread 1 tablespoon of guacamole over six pieces of toast. Layer with lettuce, tomato, bacon and turkey. Spread remaining guacamole over remaining toast; place over turkey.

Yield: 6 servings.

Nutritional Analysis: 1 sandwich equals 333 calories, 13 g fat (4 g saturated fat), 34 mg cholesterol, 1,511 mg sodium, 34 g carbohydrate, 6 g fiber, 22 g protein.

Types of Lettuce

Whenever you make sandwiches like Guacamole Turkey BLTs, leave ordinary iceberg on ice and reach for some greens that pack more of a nutritional punch!

Bibb, curly endive, escarole, green and red leaf, and romaine are all terrific choices.

The Secret to Slicing Tomatoes

The best way to cut through the skin of a tomato is with a serrated, not a straight-edged, knife.

For slices that will be less juicy and hold their shape better, cut a tomato vertically, from stem end to blossom end.

Fruited Pork Tenderloin (p. 160)

Liven up
ordinary weekday
dinners with a
selection of prime pork
cuts, such as chops, ribs,
tenderloin, ham and sausage.

Pleasing Pork

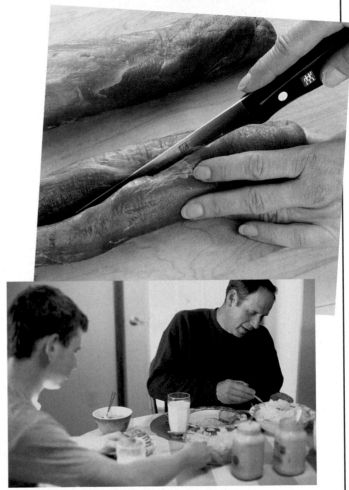

Ginger-Apple Pork Chops

PREP: 15 min.   **BAKE:** 25 min.

  6 boneless pork loin chops (1 inch thick
      and 8 ounces *each*)
  1 teaspoon salt
1/2 teaspoon pepper
  1 tablespoon vegetable oil
  1 can (21 ounces) apple pie filling
 12 gingersnaps, crumbled
  2 tablespoons cornstarch
  2 cups unsweetened apple juice

Cut a pocket in each pork chop. Sprinkle with salt and pepper. In a large skillet, brown chops in oil on both sides. Cool for 5 minutes. Combine the pie filling and gingersnaps; stuff some of the mixture into the pocket of each chop. Set remaining mixture aside.

Secure pork with toothpicks. Place in a greased 15-in. x 10-in. x 1-in. baking pan. Cover and bake at 350° for 25-30 minutes or until a meat thermometer reads 160°. Discard toothpicks.

In a small saucepan, combine cornstarch and apple juice until smooth. Stir in reserved pie filling mixture. Bring to a boil; cook and stir for 1 minute or until thickened. Serve over pork chops.

Yield: 6 servings.

Nutritional Analysis: 1 pork chop with 1/4 cup sauce equals 530 calories, 17 g fat (5 g saturated fat), 109 mg cholesterol, 594 mg sodium, 49 g carbohydrate, 1 g fiber, 44 g protein.

Sesame Green Beans (p. 267)

Cooking with Kids

Have kids help cook dinner by enlisting them to crumble the gingersnaps for this recipe. Then have them stir together the crumbled gingersnaps and apple pie filling.

While you prepare the rest of the meal, have the kids set the table.

Speedy Side Dish

In addition to Sesame Green Beans (page 267), prepare a side dish of rice pilaf to accompany these tasty chops.

In a saucepan, saute 3/4 cup chopped onion and 1/2 cup slivered almonds in 1 tablespoon butter until the onion is tender and the almonds are lightly browned.

Add 2 cups chicken broth; bring to a boil. Stir in 2 cups uncooked instant rice and cover. Remove from the heat. Let stand for 5-8 minutes or until the liquid is absorbed.

Pork Noodle Skillet

PREP/TOTAL TIME: 15 min.

1/2 pound sliced fresh mushrooms
1 cup shredded carrots
3 tablespoons butter
1 package (17 ounces) ready-to-serve pork roast in gravy
2 cups cooked egg noodles
2 tablespoons minced fresh parsley
1/4 teaspoon pepper

In a large skillet, saute mushrooms and carrots in butter for 5 minutes or until mushrooms are tender. Cut pork roast into small pieces; add pork and gravy to the skillet. Stir in the noodles, parsley and pepper. Cook for 5 minutes or until heated through.

Yield: 4 servings.

Nutritional Analysis: 1 cup equals 175 calories, 10 g fat (6 g saturated fat), 41 mg cholesterol, 104 mg sodium, 19 g carbohydrate, 2 g fiber, 5 g protein.

Preparation Pointer

This clever recipe doctors up ready-to-serve pork roast in gravy with fresh mushrooms, carrots and seasonings.

Look for cooked pork roast in gravy in your store's convenience meat section.

Porcini Ham Risotto

PREP/TOTAL TIME: 30 min.

1	package (1 ounce) dried porcini mushrooms
2	cups boiling water
1/2	cup chopped shallots
1	teaspoon minced garlic
1/3	cup butter, cubed
1-1/2	cups uncooked arborio rice
1	cup white wine
3	cans (14-1/2 ounces *each*) chicken broth, warmed
1-1/2	cups diced fully cooked ham
5	ounces fontinella cheese, shredded
1/2	teaspoon salt
1/8	teaspoon white pepper

In a large bowl, soak mushrooms in boiling water for 5 minutes or until completely hydrated; drain. In a Dutch oven, saute the mushrooms, shallots and garlic in butter for 3-4 minutes or until tender.

Stir in rice until completely coated with butter. Add wine; cook and stir for 2 minutes or until wine is absorbed. Add one can of broth; cook and stir until broth is absorbed. Repeat with remaining broth, adding one can at a time. Stir in the ham, cheese, salt and pepper; cook until cheese is melted and mixture is heated through.

Yield: 8 servings.

Nutritional Analysis: 1 cup equals 363 calories, 16 g fat (9 g saturated fat), 53 mg cholesterol, 1,348 mg sodium, 35 g carbohydrate, 1 g fiber, 14 g protein.

Pleasing Pork

Learn About Fontinella

Fontinella is a semi-soft to hard cheese that can be found in the specialty cheese section of your local grocery store. The flavor can range from mild to sharp, depending on the age of the cheese.

Porcini Mushroom Pointer

Unlike fresh mushrooms, dried mushrooms such as porcini can be kept in the pantry for exciting recipes like this.

Ham 'n' Brie Sandwiches

PREP/TOTAL TIME: 20 min.

1/3	cup mayonnaise
2	teaspoons Dijon mustard
1/2	teaspoon minced garlic
1/2	teaspoon white wine vinegar
1	package (8 ounces) round Brie cheese
6	English muffins, split
3/4	pound shaved deli ham
12	slices tomato

In a small bowl, combine the mayonnaise, mustard, garlic and vinegar until blended. Cut the Brie horizontally into three rounds; cut each round into eight wedges.

Place English muffins, cut side up, in a foil-lined 15-in. x 10-in. x 1-in. baking pan. Broil 3-4 in. from the heat for 2 minutes or until lightly toasted.

Spread muffins with mayonnaise mixture. Layer with ham, tomato and cheese wedges. Broil 3-4 in. from the heat for 5 minutes or until cheese is melted.

Yield: 6 servings.

Nutritional Analysis: 2 sandwich halves equals 419 calories, 24 g fat (9 g saturated fat), 69 mg cholesterol, 1,379 mg sodium, 29 g carbohydrate, 2 g fiber, 22 g protein.

Mayo Versus Salad Dressing

Mayonnaise is a thick, creamy sauce made with oil, egg yolks, lemon juice or vinegar and seasonings. Salad dressing doesn't contain egg yolks and is generally sweeter.

Mayonnaise was invented in 1756 by the French chef of the Duc de Richelieu. After the Duc beat the British at Port Mahon, his chef created a victory feast that was to include a sauce made of cream and eggs. Realizing that there was no cream in the kitchen, the chef substituted olive oil for the cream, and a new culinary creation was born. The chef named the new sauce "Mahonnaise" in honor of the Duc's victory.

Jicama-Radish Spinach Salad (p. 271)

Moo Shu Pork

PREP/TOTAL TIME: 20 min.

- 1 tablespoon cornstarch
- 1/4 cup cold water
- 2 tablespoons reduced-sodium soy sauce
- 2 teaspoons minced fresh gingerroot
- 5 boneless pork loin chops (4 ounces *each*), cut into thin strips
- 1 teaspoon minced garlic
- 2 teaspoons sesame oil
- 1/4 cup hoisin sauce
- 3 cups coleslaw mix with carrots
- 8 flour tortillas (8 inches), warmed

In a small bowl, combine the cornstarch, water, soy sauce and ginger until blended; set aside. In a large skillet, saute pork and garlic in oil for 3-5 minutes or until meat is no longer pink.

Stir cornstarch mixture and add to the skillet. Bring to a boil; cook and stir for 1-2 minutes or until thickened. Stir in hoisin sauce. Add coleslaw mix; stir to coat. Spoon about 1/2 cup pork mixture into the center of each tortilla; roll up tightly.

Yield: 4 servings.

Nutritional Analysis: 1 serving equals 564 calories, 17 g fat (4 g saturated fat), 69 mg cholesterol, 1,111 mg sodium, 63 g carbohydrate, 2 g fiber, 38 g protein.

Make It Moo Shu!

Moo Shu is a Chinese stir-fry dish usually containing shredded pork, chicken or beef, scallions, scrambled eggs and seasonings. The mixture is then rolled in small thin pancakes and topped with a plum or hoisin sauce. This egg-less version uses ready-to-eat flour tortillas.

What Is Hoisin Sauce?

Hoisin is a Chinese cooking condiment made from soybeans, garlic, chilies and seasonings, resulting in a thick, reddish-brown, sweet-and-spicy sauce.

Microwave Pork and Peas

PREP/TOTAL TIME: 25 min.

2 tablespoons vegetable oil
1 pound boneless pork, cut into 1/4-inch strips
2 tablespoons soy sauce
1/8 teaspoon garlic powder
1 package (6 ounces) frozen snow peas, thawed
1 cup thinly sliced green onions
2 tablespoons cornstarch
1 cup beef broth
Hot cooked rice, optional

In a 2-qt. microwave-safe dish, heat oil at 70% power for 2 minutes. Add the pork, soy sauce and garlic powder; toss to coat. Cover and microwave on high for 7-8 minutes or until meat is no longer pink.

Stir in peas and onions. Cover and microwave at 70% power for 3 minutes. Combine the cornstarch and broth until smooth; stir into pork mixture. Cover and microwave on high for 2 minutes; stir. Cover and microwave 4-5 minutes longer or until thickened, stirring every minute. Serve over rice if desired.

Editor's Note: This recipe was tested in a 1,100-watt microwave.

Yield: 4 servings.

Nutritional Analysis: 1 cup pork mixture (calculated without rice) equals 277 calories, 14 g fat (3 g saturated fat), 67 mg cholesterol, 723 mg sodium, 9 g carbohydrate, 2 g fiber, 26 g protein.

Preparation Pointer

A 14-1/2-ounce can of beef broth yields about 1-3/4 cups. Use 1 cup in this recipe, then refrigerate the leftovers in an airtight container for up to a few days. Use it to make Spicy Pork Chili on page 163.

Chili Chops

PREP/TOTAL TIME: 30 min.

4   bone-in pork loin chops (1/2 inch thick
     and 6 ounces *each*)
4   slices onion (1/4 inch thick)
4   slices green pepper (1/4 inch thick)
1   bottle (12 ounces) chili sauce

Place the pork chops in a greased 9-in. square baking dish. Top with the onion, green pepper and chili sauce. Cover and bake at 350° for 20-30 minutes or until meat juices run clear.

Yield: 4 servings.

Nutritional Analysis: 1 serving equals 418 calories, 18 g fat (7 g saturated fat), 111 mg cholesterol, 1,457 mg sodium, 26 g carbohydrate, trace fiber, 36 g protein.

Chose Choice Chops

When out shopping, you've likely noticed there are several types of pork chops to chose from.

Loin pork chops are tender, prime chops with a characteristic T-bone on one side.

Butterfly loin chops are boneless chops cut from the eye of the loin.

Rib pork chops are tender, prime chops. Sirloin, top loin and loin blade chops are value-priced pork chops.

The most tender chops are cut from the loin, and slightly less tender chops come from the ribs.

Pork chop meat should be reddish pink. Avoid cutlets that have a brown or greenish tinge or that are slimy or have an odor.

Keep raw pork chops in their original wrapping and store in the refrigerator for 2 to 3 days or freeze for up to 6 months.

Fruited Pork Tenderloin

PREP: 15 min.   **BAKE:** 30 min.

1/4 cup dried cranberries
1/4 cup chopped dried apricots
3/4 cup boiling water
1/2 cup chopped onion
  2 tablespoons butter
1/2 cup coarsely chopped pecans
  2 pork tenderloins (1 pound *each*)
1/4 teaspoon salt
1/4 teaspoon pepper
1/3 cup apricot preserves, warmed, *divided*

Place cranberries and apricots in a bowl; add boiling water. Soak for 8 minutes; drain. In a small skillet, saute the onion in butter until tender. Remove from the heat. Stir in the pecans, cranberries and apricots.

Make a lengthwise slit down the center of each tenderloin, cutting two-thirds of the way through the meat. Place on a greased rack in a broiler pan; open tenderloins so they lie flat. Sprinkle with salt and pepper. Brush with half of the preserves; top with fruit mixture. Bake at 375° for 30-35 minutes or until a meat thermometer reads 160°. Drizzle with remaining preserves.

Yield: 6 servings.

Nutritional Analysis: 5 ounces cooked pork with 1 tablespoon fruit mixture equals 354 calories, 16 g fat (5 g saturated fat), 94 mg cholesterol, 208 mg sodium, 22 g carbohydrate, 2 g fiber, 31 g protein.

Pork Tenderloin Lesson

Pork tenderloin is one of the leanest meats available. And according to the National Pork Producers, it's nearly as low in saturated fat as chicken breasts.

Since pork tenderloin has very little fat, a small amount can go a long way. When purchasing, look for meat that is firm and grayish pink in color. For best flavor and tenderness, meat should have a small amount of marbling.

Stock up on pork tenderloin when it's on sale. Use within 3 to 5 days or freeze up to 1 year.

Time-Saving Tip

Get a head start on dinner by preparing the fruit and nut mixture for this recipe the night before. Cover tightly and refrigerate.

Sweet Potatoes 'n' Pears (p. 277)

Pleasing **Pork**

Pleasing **Pork**

Spicy Pork Chili

PREP: 10 min.   **COOK:** 6 hours

2   **pounds boneless pork, cut into 1/2-inch cubes**
1   **tablespoon vegetable oil**
1   **can (28 ounces) crushed tomatoes**
2   **cups frozen corn**
1   **can (15 ounces) black beans, rinsed and drained**
1   **cup chopped onion**
1   **cup beef broth**
1   **can (4 ounces) chopped green chilies**
1   **tablespoon chili powder**
1   **teaspoon minced garlic**
1/2   **teaspoon salt**
1/2   **teaspoon cayenne pepper**
1/2   **teaspoon pepper**
1/4   **cup minced fresh cilantro**
Shredded cheddar cheese, optional

In a large skillet, cook pork in oil over medium-high heat for 5-6 minutes or until browned. Transfer pork and drippings to a 5-qt. slow cooker.

Stir in the tomatoes, corn, beans, onion, broth, chilies, chili powder, garlic, salt, cayenne and pepper. Cover and cook on low for 6 hours or until pork is tender. Stir in cilantro. Serve with cheese if desired.

Yield: 6 servings.

Nutritional Analysis: 1-3/4 cups chili (calculated without cheese) equals 400 calories, 12 g fat (4 g saturated fat), 89 mg cholesterol, 798 mg sodium, 35 g carbohydrate, 8 g fiber, 39 g protein.

Get to Know Cilantro

The leaves of a cilantro plant give a distinctive taste to Mexican and Southwest-style cooking. (Coriander comes from the seeds of the same plant but has a much different flavor.)

If you and your family aren't fond of cilantro's flavor, use half of the amount or substitute parsley.

What Type of Pork to Use?

When a recipe (like this Spicy Pork Chili) calls for cubed boneless pork, you can use pork tenderloin, boneless pork roast or boneless pork chops.

Sausage Polenta Bake

PREP: 5 min.   **BAKE:** 35 min. + standing

- 1-1/4 cups yellow cornmeal
- 1/2 teaspoon salt
- 4 cups boiling water
- 1/4 cup grated Parmesan cheese
- 1/2 pound bulk sweet Italian sausage
- 1/2 pound bulk hot Italian sausage
- 1 teaspoon olive oil
- 1 jar (26 ounces) garden-style spaghetti sauce
- 1-1/2 cups (6 ounces) shredded mozzarella cheese

In a large saucepan, combine cornmeal and salt. Gradually add boiling water, whisking constantly. Cook and stir over medium heat for 5 minutes or until mixture comes to a boil. Remove from the heat. Stir in Parmesan cheese.

Spread polenta into a greased 13-in. x 9-in. x 2-in. baking dish. Bake, uncovered, at 350° for 20 minutes. Meanwhile, in a large skillet, cook sausage in oil over medium heat for 5 minutes or until no longer pink; drain. Add spaghetti sauce; cook for 5 minutes or until heated through.

Spread over polenta; sprinkle with mozzarella cheese. Bake 12-15 minutes longer or until cheese is melted. Let stand for 15 minutes before cutting.

Yield: 8 servings.

Nutritional Analysis: 1 serving equals 311 calories, 16 g fat (6 g saturated fat), 44 mg cholesterol, 887 mg sodium, 28 g carbohydrate, 4 g fiber, 14 g protein.

Purchased Polenta Saves Time

Instead of making polenta from scratch for this recipe, purchase two 1-pound packages of polenta and cut into 1/2-in. slices. Place in a single layer in a greased 13-in. x 9-in. x 2-in. baking pan. Bake, uncovered, at 350° for 15-20 minutes or until heated through. Top with the spaghetti sauce mixture and cheese; bake as directed.

Pear 'n' Fennel Pork

PREP/TOTAL TIME: 25 min.

- 4 **boneless butterflied pork chops (1/2 inch thick and 6 ounces *each*)**
- 1/2 **teaspoon salt**
- 1/4 **teaspoon pepper**
- 1 **tablespoon olive oil**
- 1 **cup sliced onion**
- 1 **cup sliced fennel bulb**
- 1 **tablespoon butter**
- 2 **tablespoons cornstarch**
- 2 **cups pear nectar**
- 3 **tablespoons maple syrup**
- 1/2 **to 1 teaspoon ground nutmeg**

Sprinkle pork chops with salt and pepper. In a large skillet, cook chops in oil over medium-high heat for 4-5 minutes on each side or until juices run clear; drain. Set chops aside and keep warm.

In the same skillet, saute the onion and fennel in butter until crisp-tender. In a small bowl, combine the cornstarch, pear nectar, syrup and nutmeg until smooth; add to the skillet. Bring to a boil; cook and stir for 2 minutes or until thickened. Serve over pork chops.

Yield: 4 servings.

Nutritional Analysis: 1 pork chop with 1/2 cup sauce equals 431 calories, 16 g fat (6 g saturated fat), 90 mg cholesterol, 390 mg sodium, 38 g carbohydrate, 2 g fiber, 33 g protein.

Fresh Fennel Facts

Fennel is available year-round, but fall and winter are the peak seasons. It has a large bulbous base and pale green stems with wispy foliage. Often mislabeled as sweet anise, it has a sweeter and more delicate flavor than anise.

Purchase clean, crisp bulbs with no brown spots. Any attached greens will be soft but should have a fresh green color. Tightly wrap fennel in a plastic bag and refrigerate up to 5 days.

Before using, wash, trim the base and remove the stalks and greens.

Tenderloin with Cherry Sauce

PREP/TOTAL TIME: 30 min.

- **1 tablespoon cornstarch**
- **1-1/2 cups cranberry juice**
- **2 teaspoons Dijon mustard**
- **1 pork tenderloin (1-1/2 pounds), thinly sliced**
- **2 teaspoons lemon-pepper seasoning**
- **3 tablespoons butter**
- **1 cup dried cherries**
- **3 tablespoons cherry preserves**

In a small bowl, combine the cornstarch, cranberry juice and mustard until smooth; set aside. Sprinkle pork with lemon-pepper. In a large skillet, cook pork in butter for 4-5 minutes on each side or until no longer pink. Remove pork and keep warm.

Stir cornstarch mixture and add to the skillet. Bring to a boil. Add cherries and preserves; cook and stir for 2 minutes or until thickened. Return pork to the pan; cook for 2 minutes or until heated through.

Yield: 4 servings.

Nutritional Analysis: 1 serving equals 477 calories, 15 g fat (7 g saturated fat), 118 mg cholesterol, 451 mg sodium, 50 g carbohydrate, 1 g fiber, 35 g protein.

Speedy Side Dishes

Cranberry Couscous (page 258) is a flavorful fruity dish to accompany Tenderloin with Cherry Sauce. For a vegetable to serve on the side, make Honey-Glazed Carrots.

Place one 16-ounce package of baby carrots and 1 tablespoon water in a 1-1/2-qt. microwave-safe dish. Cover and microwave on high for 5-7 minutes or until crisp-tender. Melt 2 tablespoons butter in a skillet; stir in 2 tablespoons honey and 1 tablespoon lemon juice. Cook over low heat for 5 minutes, stirring constantly. Add carrots; cook and stir for 2 minutes or until glazed. (This recipe was tested in an 850-watt microwave.)

Cranberry Couscous (p. 258)

Pleasing **Pork**

Mushroom Prosciutto Pasta

PREP/TOTAL TIME: 30 min.

4 **cups uncooked penne** *or* **medium tube pasta**
1/2 **pound sliced fresh mushrooms**
1/4 **cup chopped onion**
2 **tablespoons butter**
10 **thin slices prosciutto, chopped**
2 **teaspoons cornstarch**
2 **cups heavy whipping cream**
1/2 **cup minced fresh parsley**
1/4 **teaspoon pepper**
Shredded Parmesan cheese, optional

Substitution Secrets

Prosciutto is an aged, dry-cured spiced Italian ham. If it's not available at your deli counter, buy 10 thin slices of fully cooked ham and chop it.

The sauce for Mushroom Prosciutto Pasta is simple to make. But for even faster preparation, substitute prepared Alfredo sauce instead.

Cook pasta according to package directions. Meanwhile, in a large skillet, saute the mushrooms and onion in butter until tender. Add prosciutto; saute for 3 minutes.

In a bowl, combine the cornstarch and cream until smooth; stir into the skillet. Add parsley and pepper. Bring to a boil; cook and stir for 2 minutes or until thickened. Drain pasta; add to the skillet and stir to coat. Sprinkle with Parmesan cheese if desired.

Yield: 6 servings.

Nutritional Analysis: 1-1/3 cups pasta mixture (calculated without cheese) equals 622 calories, 38 g fat (22 g saturated fat), 144 mg cholesterol, 622 mg sodium, 54 g carbohydrate, 3 g fiber, 19 g protein.

Ham with Mango

PREP/TOTAL TIME: 20 min.

1   cup chopped peeled mango
1/2 cup chopped sweet red pepper
1/4 cup chopped seeded tomato
3   green onions, sliced
2   tablespoons minced fresh
     cilantro
1/8 teaspoon salt
2   tablespoons lime juice
1   teaspoon chili powder
1/2 teaspoon ground cumin
1/4 teaspoon ground coriander
1/8 teaspoon cayenne pepper
1   bone-in fully cooked ham steak
     (1 pound and 1/2 inch thick)

For salsa, in a bowl, combine the mango, red pepper, tomato, onions, cilantro and salt. Sprinkle with lime juice and toss to combine; set aside.

Combine the chili powder, cumin, coriander and cayenne; sprinkle half over one side of ham steak. Cut into four pieces. In a large skillet coated with nonstick cooking spray, cook the ham, seasoned side down, over medium heat for 1-2 minutes or until browned. Sprinkle with remaining seasoning. Turn and cook 1-2 minutes longer or until browned. Serve with salsa.

Yield: 4 servings.

Nutritional Analysis: 1 piece of ham with 1/2 cup salsa equals 267 calories, 15 g fat (5 g saturated fat), 59 mg cholesterol, 1,610 mg sodium, 11 g carbohydrate, 2 g fiber, 23 g protein.

Buying and Storing Mangoes

Mangoes have a long growing season and are available from January through August, with June being their peak month.

Purchase mangoes that are somewhat soft with uniformly smooth skin. Mangoes with some green areas will ripen at room temperature.

Once ripened, mangoes should be stored in the refrigerator and used within a few days.

Pleasing **Pork**

Zesty Grilled Chops

PREP: 5 min. + marinating   **GRILL:** 10 min.

3/4 cup soy sauce
1/4 cup lemon juice
1 tablespoon brown sugar
1 tablespoon chili sauce
1/4 teaspoon garlic powder
6 bone-in pork loin chops (8 ounces *each*)

In a large resealable plastic bag, combine the soy sauce, lemon juice, brown sugar, chili sauce and garlic powder. Remove 1/4 cup for basting and refrigerate. Add pork chops to the remaining marinade; turn to coat. Cover and refrigerate for 3 hours or overnight, turning once.

Drain and discard marinade from chops. Grill, covered, over medium-hot heat for 4 minutes. Turn; baste with reserved marinade. Grill 4-7 minutes longer or until juices run clear.

Yield: 6 servings.

Nutritional Analysis: 1 serving equals 341 calories, 18 g fat (7 g saturated fat), 111 mg cholesterol, 1,249 mg sodium, 2 g carbohydrate, trace fiber, 39 g protein.

On-the-Grill Side Dish

Broccoli with Red Pepper (page 261) can be prepared on the stovetop while Zesty Grilled Chops are cooking.

For a change of pace, make a vegetable side dish on the grill! Cut 1 medium green pepper, 1 medium sweet red pepper and 2 medium zucchini into julienne strips. Place on a double layer of heavy-duty foil (about 18 in. x 15 in.). Dot with 1 tablespoon butter; drizzle with 2 teaspoons soy sauce. Grill, covered, over medium heat for 10-15 minutes or until vegetables are crisp-tender.

Thicker Is Better

When buying bone-in pork chops, try to find cuts at least 3/4 inch or thicker. The meat closest to the bone takes longer to cook, so thinner chops tend to overcook and dry out before the area by the bone is cooked.

Broccoli with Red Pepper (p. 261)

Bacon Avocado Wraps

PREP/TOTAL TIME: 15 min.

1/3 cup mayonnaise
2 tablespoons chipotle sauce
1 tablespoon sour cream
1 package (2.1 ounces) ready-to-serve fully cooked bacon
4 flour tortillas (8 inches)
4 large lettuce leaves
1 large tomato, sliced
2 medium ripe avocados, peeled and sliced

In a small bowl, combine the mayonnaise, chipotle sauce and sour cream until smooth. Heat bacon according to package directions. Spread chipotle mayonnaise over tortillas; layer with lettuce, tomato, bacon and avocados. Roll up tightly.

Editor's Note: This recipe was tested with San Marcos brand chipotle sauce. It can be found in the Mexican section of your grocery store.

Yield: 4 servings.

Nutritional Analysis: 1 wrap equals 527 calories, 39 g fat (7 g saturated fat), 9 mg cholesterol, 584 mg sodium, 35 g carbohydrate, 5 g fiber, 12 g protein.

A Chipotle Primer

Chipotle (chi-POHT-lay) is the common spelling of the word "chilpotle," which means smoked chile.

Chipotle peppers are fully ripe red jalapenos that have been smoked, resulting in a fabulous flavor that's neither too hot nor too mild.

Other Ways to Use Chipotle Sauce

One bottle of chipotle sauce can go a long way. Don't let it go to waste …use some to make Beef Tostadas on page 17!

You can also use leftover chipotle sauce to liven up bottled salsa or an ordinary meat loaf recipe, to marinate boneless skinless chicken breasts and to baste steaks, chops and kabobs.

Pleasing **Pork**

Canadian Bacon Pizza

PREP/TOTAL TIME: 25 min.

   1 loaf (1 pound) French bread
 1/4 cup butter, melted
   2 cups marinara sauce
  16 slices Canadian bacon
   1 can (20 ounces) unsweetened pineapple tidbits,
       drained
 1/2 cup chopped green pepper
 1/4 cup chopped green onions
   2 cups (8 ounces) shredded mozzarella cheese

Cut bread in half lengthwise, then in half widthwise. Place cut side up in a foil-lined 15-in. x 10-in. x 1-in. baking pan. Brush with butter. Bake at 450° for 5 minutes or until lightly browned.

Spread marinara sauce over bread. Top with Canadian bacon, pineapple, green pepper, onions and cheese. Bake for 8-10 minutes or until cheese is melted. Cut each piece in half.

Yield: 8 servings.

Nutritional Analysis: 1 piece equals 440 calories, 17 g fat (9 g saturated fat), 64 mg cholesterol, 1,343 mg sodium, 48 g carbohydrate, 4 g fiber, 23 g protein.

Canadian Bacon Basics

Canadian bacon (known as back bacon in Canada) comes from the eye of the loin in the middle of the back of the animal. It's not really bacon, because it is much leaner and has the flavor and consistency of ham. Use Canadian bacon as you would ham, rather than as bacon.

Substitution Secrets

The great thing about pizza is you can be creative and come up with a host of tasty combinations.

In place of French bread, substitute an Italian bread shell, one tube refrigerated pizza crust or even home-made pizza crust. Not fond of Canadian bacon? Use ham or pepperoni.

No green pepper on hand? Simply leave it off or add some canned sliced mushrooms. Replace the mozzarella cheese with Monterey Jack or sprinkle grated Romano cheese over the top.

Pork Chops Mole

PREP/TOTAL TIME: 30 min.

4   boneless pork loin chops (1 inch thick
     and 6 ounces *each*)
2   tablespoons olive oil, *divided*
1   cup sliced onion
1   cup julienned green pepper
1   can (14-1/2 ounces) Mexican diced tomatoes
1   to 2 tablespoons mole sauce *or* paste
Hot cooked rice, optional

In a large skillet over medium-high heat, brown pork chops in 1 tablespoon oil on both sides; remove and set aside. In the same skillet, saute the onion and green pepper in remaining oil until crisp-tender.

Add tomatoes and mole sauce; stir to combine. Return pork chops to the pan. Cover and cook for 10 minutes or until meat is no longer pink. Serve with rice if desired.

Yield: 4 servings.

Nutritional Analysis: 1 pork chop with 1/2 cup sauce (calculated without rice) equals 351 calories, 17 g fat (4 g saturated fat), 82 mg cholesterol, 553 mg sodium, 13 g carbohydrate, 3 g fiber, 34 g protein.

Preparation Pointer

Mole sauce or paste, a spicy sauce made with chocolate, cinnamon, dried red pepper and other ingredients, can be found in the Mexican section of your local supermarket.

Speedy Side Dish

Instead of ordinary rice, consider serving Pork Chops Mole with couscous.

Couscous is small bits of semolina (coarsely ground wheat flour). It has a slightly nutty flavor, making it more tasty than rice. It's easy to cook in just a few minutes.

Cheesy Wild Rice Soup

PREP/TOTAL TIME: 25 min.

- 1 package (6.2 ounces) fast-cooking long grain and wild rice mix
- 4 cups milk
- 1 can (10-3/4 ounces) condensed cream of potato soup, undiluted
- 8 ounces process cheese (Velveeta), cubed
- 1/2 pound sliced bacon, cooked and crumbled

In a large saucepan, prepare rice according to package directions. Stir in the milk, soup and cheese. Cook and stir until cheese is melted. Garnish with bacon.

Yield: 8 servings.

Nutritional Analysis: 1 cup equals 464 calories, 29 g fat (14 g saturated fat), 70 mg cholesterol, 1,492 mg sodium, 29 g carbohydrate, 1 g fiber, 21 g protein.

Soup and Salad Supper

Complement steaming bowls of soup with a cool, crisp side salad. Supermarkets offer a variety of salad kits with dressings like Caesar, Romano and ranch. Embellish them by tossing in a variety of your favorite fresh vegetables.

Any leftover salad should be eaten within 2 days and before the "Best If Used By" date on the package.

Roasted Pepper Tortellini

PREP/TOTAL TIME: 25 min.

- 1 package (20 ounces) refrigerated cheese tortellini
- 5 Italian sausage links
- 2 tablespoons olive oil
- 1 jar (15-1/2 ounces) roasted sweet red peppers, drained
- 1 can (15 ounces) pizza sauce
- 1 cup (4 ounces) shredded mozzarella cheese
- 2 tablespoons shredded Parmesan cheese

Cook tortellini according to package directions. Meanwhile, in a large skillet, cook sausage in oil over medium heat until no longer pink; drain. Cut into 1/4-in. slices.

Place the red peppers in a blender or food processor; cover and process until smooth. Drain tortellini. Add the tortellini, pureed peppers and pizza sauce to the skillet; stir to combine. Cook for 5 minutes or until heated through. Sprinkle with cheeses; cover and heat until cheese is melted.

Yield: 6 servings.

Nutritional Analysis: 1-1/3 cups equals 521 calories, 28 g fat (10 g saturated fat), 74 mg cholesterol, 1,249 mg sodium, 43 g carbohydrate, 4 g fiber, 26 g protein.

Italian Sausage Tips

Italian sausage links come in several varieties, such as mild (a balanced blend of herbs and spices), hot (featuring zesty seasonings such as crushed red pepper flakes) and sweet (with a hint of fresh sweet basil). Select a flavor your family will savor.

Italian sausage will stay fresh in the refrigerator for 3 days. For longer storage, freeze for up to 1 month.

Substitution Secret

Stores carry many types of refrigerated cheese tortellini, including herb, spinach, three-cheese and tricolored. Any can be used in this recipe. Or keep a box of dried tortellini in your pantry for a satisfying meal at a moment's notice.

Pretty Ham Primavera

PREP/TOTAL TIME: 15 min.

- 1/2 pound sliced fresh mushrooms
- 1/3 cup chopped onion
- 2 tablespoons olive oil
- 2 tablespoons all-purpose flour
- 2 teaspoons Italian seasoning
- 2 teaspoons chicken bouillon granules
- 1/2 teaspoon salt
- 1/8 teaspoon pepper
- 2 cups milk
- 1 package (7 ounces) thin spaghetti, cooked and drained
- 2 cups cubed fully cooked ham
- 1 package (10 ounces) frozen peas, thawed

Grated Parmesan cheese, optional

In a large skillet, saute the mushrooms and onion in oil until tender. Stir in the flour, Italian seasoning, bouillon, salt and pepper until smooth.

Gradually add the milk, stirring constantly. Bring to a boil; cook and stir for 2 minutes or until thickened. Stir in the spaghetti, ham and peas; heat through. Sprinkle with the Parmesan cheese if desired.

Yield: 4 servings.

Nutritional Analysis: 1-1/2 cups pasta mixture (calculated without cheese) equals 526 calories, 18 g fat (6 g saturated fat), 54 mg cholesterol, 1,755 mg sodium, 62 g carbohydrate, 6 g fiber, 29 g protein.

Keep Ham Handy

You can find packages of cubed cooked ham near the processed meats in your grocery store. It's convenient to have some in the refrigerator for this entree or to stir into scrambled eggs at breakfast.

If you prepare a ham on a weekend, you can refrigerate leftovers for 3 days or freeze them for up to 2 months. To keep it moist, be sure to wrap tightly in plastic wrap, then place in a resealable plastic bag.

Italian Sausage Soup

PREP: 10 min.   **COOK:** 40 min.

- 1 **can (49-1/2 ounces) chicken broth**
- 2 **cups cut fresh green beans**
- 1 **can (15 ounces) cannellini** *or* **white kidney beans, rinsed and drained**
- 1 **can (14-1/2 ounces) Italian diced tomatoes**
- 1 **cup chopped onion**
- 1 **cup chopped celery**
- 1 **cup chopped fennel bulb**
- 1 **can (6 ounces) tomato paste**
- 1 **teaspoon dried oregano**
- 1/2 **teaspoon white pepper**
- 5 **Italian sausage links**
- 1 **tablespoon olive oil**
- 3 **cups coarsely chopped fresh spinach**

Shredded Parmesan cheese, optional

In a Dutch oven, combine the first 10 ingredients. Bring to a boil. Reduce heat; cover and simmer for 20 minutes.

Meanwhile, in a large skillet, brown sausage in oil over medium heat. Add a small amount of hot water. Cover and cook until sausage is no longer pink; drain. Cut into 1/4-in. slices and add to soup. Simmer, uncovered, for 15 minutes.

Add spinach. Simmer, uncovered, for 5 minutes or until spinach is wilted. Garnish with Parmesan cheese if desired.

Yield: 8 servings.

Nutritional Analysis: 1-1/2 cups soup (calculated without cheese) equals 266 calories, 13 g fat (4 g saturated fat), 33 mg cholesterol, 1,391 mg sodium, 23 g carbohydrate, 6 g fiber, 14 g protein.

Select Baby Spinach

When a recipe calls for fresh spinach, pick up a package of prewashed baby spinach. Its leaves (and even stems) are soft and tender with a mild flavor.

Look for baby spinach with deep green leaves that are dry and free of bruising.

If you have more spinach than you can use, steam it until wilted, squeeze out the excess water, then freeze. Use it for recipes calling for frozen chopped spinach.

Baby Back Ribs

PREP: 5 min.   **COOK:** 6 hours 15 min.

2-1/2   pounds pork baby back ribs, cut into eight pieces
   5   cups water
   1   medium onion, sliced
   2   celery ribs, cut in half
   2   teaspoons minced garlic, *divided*
   1   teaspoon whole peppercorns
 1/2   cup barbecue sauce
 1/4   cup plum sauce
Dash hot pepper sauce

Place the ribs in a 5-qt. slow cooker. Add the water, onion, celery, 1 teaspoon garlic and peppercorns. Cover and cook on low for 6 hours or until meat is tender.

In a small saucepan, combine the barbecue sauce, plum sauce, hot pepper sauce and remaining garlic. Cook and stir over medium heat for 5 minutes or until heated through. Remove ribs. Discard cooking juices and vegetables.

Coat grill rack with nonstick cooking spray before starting the grill. Brush ribs with sauce. Grill, uncovered, over medium-low heat for 8-10 minutes or until browned, turning occasionally and brushing with remaining sauce.

Yield: 4 servings.

Nutritional Analysis: 1 serving equals 555 calories, 39 g fat (14 g saturated fat), 153 mg cholesterol, 500 mg sodium, 15 g carbohydrate, 1 g fiber, 33 g protein.

Pointers for Buying Ribs

Baby back ribs (also sold as loin back ribs) come from the loin of the hog. They are less meaty and less fatty than spareribs but much more tender.

Look for meaty ribs with no large areas of fat and with little exposed bones. If possible, avoid buying frozen or previously frozen ribs. Plan on about 1-1/2 servings for every pound of ribs.

Speedy Side Dish

Just before putting Baby Back Ribs on the grill, start cooking the potatoes for Smashed Red Potatoes (page 275) to serve on the side.

Smashed Red Potatoes (p. 275)

Breaded Pork Chops

PREP/TOTAL TIME: 30 min.

 1 **egg**
3/4 **cup seasoned bread crumbs**
 4 **bone-in pork loin chops (1/2 inch thick
      and 6 ounces** *each***)**
 1 **carton (8 ounces) spreadable chive and onion
      cream cheese**
 3 **tablespoons chicken broth**
 2 **tablespoons milk**

In a shallow bowl, beat the egg. Place the bread crumbs in another shallow bowl. Dip pork chops into egg, then coat with crumbs. Place in a greased 15-in. x 10-in. x 1-in. baking pan. Bake, uncovered, at 350° for 25-30 minutes or until a meat thermometer reads 160°.

In a small saucepan, combine the cream cheese, broth and milk. Cook and stir over medium heat for 5 minutes or until smooth and blended. Serve with pork chops.

Yield: 4 servings.

Nutritional Analysis: 1 pork chop with 1/4 cup sauce equals 547 calories, 35 g fat (19 g saturated fat), 192 mg cholesterol, 690 mg sodium, 19 g carbohydrate, 1 g fiber, 34 g protein.

Preparation Pointer

After opening a can of ready-to-use chicken broth for this recipe, freeze the rest in 1/2-cup portions and use to make Basil Cream Chicken (page 115), Catfish in Ginger Sauce (page 242), Cauliflower Au Gratin (page 270) or Saucy Turkey (page 129).

Speedy Side Dishes

Cider-Glazed Carrots (page 287) add beautiful color to the plate when served with Breaded Pork Chops.

For an additional side dish, pop some potatoes in the microwave! Scrub and pierce 4 medium potatoes (about 1-1/3 pounds). Place on a microwave-safe plate. Microwave, uncovered, on high for 12-14 minutes or until tender, turning once. Serve with butter and sour cream. (This recipe was tested in an 850-watt microwave.)

Cider-Glazed Carrots (p. 287)

Teriyaki Pulled Pork Sandwiches

PREP: 10 min. **COOK:** 8 hours

1 boneless pork shoulder roast (3 pounds), trimmed
2 teaspoons olive oil
1 cup finely chopped onion
1 cup teriyaki sauce, *divided*
1/2 cup unsweetened pineapple juice
3 tablespoons all-purpose flour
6 whole wheat hamburger buns, split
1 can (20 ounces) sliced pineapple, drained

In a large skillet, brown roast in oil over medium-high heat. Cut in half; place in a 5-qt. slow cooker. Add the onion, 1/2 cup teriyaki sauce and pineapple juice. Cover and cook on low for 7-8 hours or until meat is tender.

Remove roast; set aside. In a small bowl, combine the flour and remaining teriyaki sauce until smooth; stir into cooking juices. Cover and cook on high for 30-40 minutes or until thickened. Shred meat with two forks; return to the slow cooker and heat through. Spoon 1/2 cup onto each bun; top with a slice of pineapple.

Yield: 8 servings.

Nutritional Analysis: 1 sandwich equals 369 calories, 13 g fat (4 g saturated fat), 70 mg cholesterol, 1,440 mg sodium, 36 g carbohydrate, 4 g fiber, 25 g protein.

Speedy Side Dishes

The day before you plan on preparing Teriyaki Pulled Pork Sandwiches, whip up Colorful Pea Salad (page 269). Cover and refrigerate overnight.

Instead of ordinary potato chips, jazz up some frozen French fries! Place 6 cups frozen shoestring potatoes on a foil-lined baking sheet. Bake at 450° for 8 minutes. Combine 1/2 cup grated Parmesan cheese, 2 teaspoons Italian seasoning and 1/2 teaspoon salt; sprinkle over potatoes and mix gently. Bake 4-5 minutes longer or until the potatoes are brown and crisp.

Colorful Pea Salad (p. 269)

Your family won't miss the meat when they dig into these mouth-watering main courses showcasing vegetables, beans, potatoes, pasta and rice!

Oven Pancake with Veggies
(p. 212)

Make It **Meatless**

Make It
Meatless

Broccoli Bean Bake

PREP: 15 min. **BAKE:** 20 min.

6 cups fresh broccoli florets
1/3 cup chopped onion
1 teaspoon minced garlic
3 tablespoons butter, *divided*
1 can (15-1/2 ounces) great northern beans, rinsed and drained
1 jar (4 ounces) diced pimientos, drained
1 teaspoon dried oregano
1/2 teaspoon salt
1/8 teaspoon pepper
2 cups (8 ounces) shredded cheddar cheese
3 tablespoons dry bread crumbs

Place broccoli in a saucepan; add 1 in. of water. Bring to a boil. Reduce heat; cover and simmer for 5-8 minutes or until crisp-tender. Meanwhile, in a skillet, saute the onion and garlic in 1 tablespoon butter. Spread into a greased 11-in. x 7-in. x 2-in. baking dish.

Drain broccoli; place over onion mixture. Top with beans and pimientos. Sprinkle with oregano, salt, pepper, cheese and bread crumbs. Melt remaining butter; pour over the top. Bake, uncovered, at 375° for 20-25 minutes or until heated through.

Yield: 8 servings.

Nutritional Analysis: 3/4 cup equals 333 calories, 22 g fat (16 g saturated fat), 77 mg cholesterol, 728 mg sodium, 17 g carbohydrate, 5 g fiber, 18 g protein.

Preparation Pointer

One pound fresh broccoli yields about 3-1/2 cups florets.

You can also look for packages of fresh broccoli florets near the salad kits in the produce section.

Speedy Side Dish

Italian Garlic Breadsticks pair well with Broccoli Bean Bake. Here's how to make 1 dozen:

In a shallow bowl, combine 1/2 cup of grated Parmesan cheese, 2 teaspoons Italian seasoning and 1 teaspoon garlic powder. Melt 1/4 cup butter and place in another shallow bowl. Separate 1 tube (11 ounces) refrigerated breadsticks into individual pieces; dip in butter, then in cheese mixture. Twist 2-3 times and place on an ungreased baking sheet. Bake at 375° for 12-14 minutes or until golden brown.

Make It **Meatless**

Mushroom Hunter's Sauce

PREP/TOTAL TIME: 20 min.

4	cups uncooked extra-wide egg noodles
1-1/2	pounds sliced fresh mushrooms
3	tablespoons butter
1	cup dry red wine
1	tablespoon cornstarch
1-1/4	cups vegetable broth
3	tablespoons tomato paste

Cook noodles according to package directions. Meanwhile, in a large skillet, saute the mushrooms in butter until tender. Add wine. Bring to a boil; cook for 5 minutes or until sauce is reduced by half.

In a small bowl, combine the cornstarch, broth and tomato paste until smooth. Add to mushroom mixture. Bring to a boil; cook and stir for 2 minutes or until thickened. Drain noodles; serve with mushroom sauce.

Yield: 4 servings.

Nutritional Analysis: 1 cup mushroom mixture with 1 cup noodles equals 330 calories, 11 g fat (6 g saturated fat), 59 mg cholesterol, 427 mg sodium, 40 g carbohydrate, 4 g fiber, 11 g protein.

All About Mushrooms

White, crimini or shiitake mushrooms can be used in this recipe.

Purchase mushrooms that are firm and even colored with tightly closed caps. Avoid ones that are broken or have soft spots.

Prepackaged mushrooms can be refrigerated as is. When buying mushrooms in bulk, refrigerate in a brown paper bag.

Use fresh mushrooms within a few days or within a week if they are packaged and unopened. Before using, quickly rinse in cold water and pat dry.

Gnocchi with Pesto Sauce

PREP/TOTAL TIME: 20 min.

> 1 package (17.6 ounces) potato gnocchi
> 1 cup diced zucchini
> 1/2 cup chopped sweet yellow pepper
> 2 teaspoons olive oil
> 1/4 cup prepared pesto
> 1 cup chopped tomatoes

Toasted pine nuts, optional

Cook gnocchi according to package directions. Meanwhile, in a large skillet, saute the zucchini and yellow pepper in oil until crisp-tender. Drain gnocchi; add to skillet with the pesto. Gently stir until coated. Stir in tomatoes. Sprinkle with pine nuts if desired.

Yield: 4 servings.

Nutritional Analysis: 1 cup (calculated without pine nuts) equals 371 calories, 11 g fat (3 g saturated fat), 14 mg cholesterol, 671 mg sodium, 56 g carbohydrate, 4 g fiber, 12 g protein.

Simple Supper

For a main dish in mere minutes, cook a package of gnocchi, drain and top with your favorite purchased spaghetti sauce.

Substitution Secret

If you don't have pine nuts on hand, substitute sunflower kernels, pecans or any nut you like!

Portobello Mushroom Burgers

PREP: 15 min. + marinating   **GRILL:** 10 min.

1/4   cup plus 3 tablespoons olive oil, *divided*
6   tablespoons balsamic vinegar, *divided*
4   slices onion (1/4 inch thick)
1   teaspoon minced garlic
1/2   teaspoon dried basil
4   portobello mushroom caps
1   tablespoon honey
4   onion rolls, split
4   lettuce leaves
4   slices tomato
4   ounces fresh mozzarella cheese, cut into 1/4-inch slices

In a resealable plastic bag, combine 1/4 cup oil and 2 tablespoons vinegar; add onion slices. Seal bag and turn to coat; marinate for 30 minutes. Meanwhile, in a small bowl, combine the garlic, basil and remaining oil. Brush over both sides of mushroom caps; set aside.

In a small saucepan, bring honey and remaining vinegar to a boil; cook for 5 minutes or until thickened. Set aside.

Drain and discard marinade from onions. Coat grill rack with nonstick cooking spray before starting the grill. Grill onions and mushrooms over medium heat for 10-12 minutes or until tender, turning frequently. Serve on rolls with lettuce, tomato and mozzarella. Drizzle with reserved balsamic-honey sauce.

Yield: 4 servings.

Nutritional Analysis: 1 burger equals 521 calories, 33 g fat (9 g saturated fat), 22 mg cholesterol, 344 mg sodium, 43 g carbohydrate, 3 g fiber, 13 g protein.

Grilling Onion Slices

To keep the onion slices together while grilling, first secure them with several wooden toothpicks. Or cook them in a foil packet.

Substitution Secrets

If fresh mozzarella isn't available, you can use deli-sliced mozzarella instead.

For even more flavor, substitute fresh basil leaves for the lettuce.

Although onion rolls have incredible flavor that complements the portobello, you could use plain, poppy seed or sesame seed rolls.

Fettuccine with Brussels Sprouts

PREP/TOTAL TIME: 25 min.

- 8 ounces uncooked fettuccine
- 1 pound fresh brussels sprouts, cored and separated into leaves
- 1/2 cup chopped red onion
- 1/2 teaspoon minced garlic
- 1/3 cup butter, cubed
- 1 cup (4 ounces) shredded Parmesan cheese
- 3/4 cup walnut halves, toasted

Cook the fettuccine according to package directions. Meanwhile, in a large skillet, saute the brussels sprouts, onion and garlic in butter until tender. Drain fettuccine; add to the skillet and toss to coat. Sprinkle with the Parmesan cheese and walnuts.

Yield: 4 servings.

Nutritional Analysis: 2 cups equals 592 calories, 35 g fat (14 g saturated fat), 55 mg cholesterol, 541 mg sodium, 55 g carbohydrate, 8 g fiber, 22 g protein.

Preparation Pointer

This recipe calls for brussels sprouts leaves, not the whole head. To separate the leaves from the brussels sprouts, cut off the stem end to loosen the leaves. Then separate them with your fingers.

Toasting Nuts

Toasting nuts before using them in recipes intensifies their flavor and adds to the crunch. While cooking the fettuccine for this recipe, toast the walnuts in a 350° oven for 10-15 minutes, stirring occasionally.

Make It **Meatless**

Gazpacho

PREP: 20 min. + chilling

6   medium tomatoes, seeded and chopped
1   medium green pepper, chopped
1   cup chopped peeled cucumber
1   cup chopped red onion
4   cups tomato juice
1   teaspoon dried oregano
1   teaspoon dried basil
1/2   teaspoon salt
1/2   teaspoon minced garlic
1/4   teaspoon pepper
Dash hot pepper sauce
3   tablespoons snipped chives
Chopped sweet yellow pepper, optional

In a large bowl, combine the tomatoes, green pepper, cucumber and onion. In another bowl, combine the tomato juice, oregano, basil, salt, garlic, pepper and hot pepper sauce; pour over vegetables. Cover and refrigerate for at least 4 hours or overnight. Sprinkle with chives and yellow pepper if desired.

Yield: 6 servings.

Nutritional Analysis: 1-1/2 cups soup equals 80 calories, 1 g fat (trace saturated fat), 0 cholesterol, 797 mg sodium, 18 g carbohydrate, 4 g fiber, 3 g protein.

History of Gazpacho

Gazpacho is a refreshingly cold, summertime soup hailing from the Andalusia region in southern Spain. This uncooked soup is usually made from a pureed mixture of fresh tomatoes, sweet bell peppers, onions, celery, cucumber, bread crumbs, garlic, olive oil, vinegar and sometimes lemon juice.

Substitution Secret

For a spicier version of Gazpacho, replace the tomato juice with spicy hot V8 juice.

Vegetarian Reubens

PREP/TOTAL TIME: 20 min.

1 package (6 ounces) sliced baby portobello
    mushrooms
2 tablespoons olive oil, *divided*
1 package (6 ounces) fresh baby spinach
2 tablespoons butter, softened
8 slices marble rye bread
1/4 cup Thousand Island salad dressing
8 slices process Swiss cheese
1 cup sauerkraut, rinsed and well drained

In a large skillet, saute mushrooms in 1 tablespoon oil until lightly browned; remove with a slotted spoon. In the same skillet, saute spinach in remaining oil until wilted. Remove from the heat.

Spread butter over one side of each slice of bread. Place four slices, buttered side down, on a griddle. Spread with half of the salad dressing; top each with one slice of cheese, mushrooms, spinach, sauerkraut and another slice of cheese.

Spread remaining salad dressing over the unbuttered side of remaining bread; place buttered side up over cheese. Cook over medium heat until toasted on both sides.

Yield: 4 servings.

Nutritional Analysis: 1 sandwich equals 475 calories, 30 g fat (12 g saturated fat), 56 mg cholesterol, 1,446 mg sodium, 35 g carbohydrate, 6 g fiber, 18 g protein.

Lively Leftovers

This recipe calls for only 1 cup of canned sauerkraut. Refrigerate leftovers in an airtight container and use to make Reuben Chowder (page 59) within the next few days.

Once opened, keep the Thousand Island salad dressing in your refrigerator for up to 3 months. Use it to top your family's favorite salad greens and vegetables.

Substitution Secrets

If you can't find sliced portobello mushrooms in the refrigerated produce section of your local grocery store, purchase 6 ounces of portobello mushroom caps instead and slice at home.

For a little flavor variation, substitute dark rye or pumpernickel bread for the marble rye.

Brown Rice Veggie Stir-Fry

PREP/TOTAL TIME: 20 min.

2 tablespoons water
2 tablespoons reduced-sodium
   soy sauce
1 tablespoon olive oil
1 cup sliced zucchini
1 cup shredded cabbage
1/2 cup sliced fresh mushrooms
1/2 cup chopped onion
1 cup cooked brown rice
1/4 cup diced fresh tomato
1/4 cup grated carrot
2 tablespoons slivered almonds

In a large skillet or wok, combine the water, soy sauce and oil. Add the zucchini, cabbage, mushrooms and onion; stir-fry for 4-5 minutes or until crisp-tender. Add the rice, tomato and carrot; stir-fry for 2-3 minutes or until heated through. Sprinkle with almonds.

Yield: 4 servings.

Nutritional Analysis: 1-1/2 cups equals 263 calories, 11 g fat (1 g saturated fat), 0 cholesterol, 627 mg sodium, 35 g carbohydrate, 6 g fiber, 7 g protein.

Storing Zucchini

When your grocer's produce section is blooming with a bounty of zucchini, pick some up to make Brown Rice Veggie Stir-Fry as well as Zippy Beef Bake (page 15), Zucchini Lasagna (page 30) and Crisp Side Salad (page 284).

Keep unwashed zucchini in a sealed plastic bag in your refrigerator crisper drawer for up to 4 days.

Vegetables in Puff Pastry

PREP/TOTAL TIME: 30 min.

1 package (10 ounces) frozen puff pastry shells
4 cups water
1 package (16 ounces) fresh baby carrots
1 teaspoon salt, *divided*
1 package (8 ounces) fresh sugar snap peas
1 medium leek (white portion only), sliced
1 teaspoon minced garlic
1 tablespoon butter
1 can (29 ounces) tomato puree
1 can (14-1/2 ounces) diced tomatoes, undrained
2 teaspoons sugar
2 teaspoons dried oregano
1/2 teaspoon pepper
1 package (16 ounces) frozen lima beans, thawed

Bake pastry shells according to package directions. Meanwhile, in a Dutch oven, bring the water to boil. Add carrots and 1/2 teaspoon salt. Reduce heat to medium; cook for 8-10 minutes or until tender. Add peas; cook for 1 minute. Drain and set aside.

In a large skillet, saute leek and garlic in butter until leek is crisp-tender. Add the tomato puree, tomatoes, sugar, oregano, pepper and remaining salt. Bring to a boil. Reduce heat. Add the lima beans and carrot mixture; cook for 5 minutes or until vegetables are heated through. Remove tops from pastry shells; fill with vegetable mixture.

Yield: 6 servings.

Nutritional Analysis: 1 pastry shell with 1-1/3 cups vegetable mixture equals 446 calories, 17 g fat (4 g saturated fat), 5 mg cholesterol, 721 mg sodium, 63 g carbohydrate, 12 g fiber, 13 g protein.

A Leek Lesson

Although a member of the onion family, leeks have a more subtle and sweet flavor so they don't overpower other foods.

Because leeks often contain sand between their many layers, it's important to thoroughly wash them before using.

When a recipe calls for sliced or chopped leeks, cut the leek open lengthwise down one side and rinse under cold running water, separating the leaves.

Make It **Meatless**

Creamy Basil Tortellini

PREP/TOTAL TIME: 20 min.

1   package (19 ounces) frozen cheese tortellini
1/2   cup julienned sweet red pepper
1-1/2   teaspoons minced garlic
2   tablespoons butter
2   cups heavy whipping cream
1/4   cup ground walnuts
2   tablespoons minced fresh basil
1   tablespoon chopped green onion

Cook tortellini according to package directions. Meanwhile, in a large skillet, saute red pepper and garlic in butter until pepper is crisp-tender. Stir in cream; cook for 8-10 minutes or until slightly thickened. Add the walnuts, basil and onion; heat through. Drain tortellini; add to sauce and toss to coat.

Yield: 4 servings.

Nutritional Analysis: 1 cup equals 771 calories, 61 g fat (35 g saturated fat), 199 mg cholesterol, 449 mg sodium, 42 g carbohydrate, 3 g fiber, 16 g protein.

Timely Tiramisu

Top off this Italian-style entree with a classic Italian dessert like tiramisu!

In a bowl, whisk 2 cups cold milk and 1 package (3.4 ounces) instant vanilla pudding mix for 2 minutes or until thickened. In a small bowl, beat 1 cup heavy whipping cream until it begins to thicken. Add 3 tablespoons confectioners' sugar; beat until soft peaks form. Fold into pudding; refrigerate.

Split 9 ladyfingers and place cut side up in an 11-in. x 7-in. x 2-in. dish. Dissolve 2-1/2 teaspoons instant coffee granules in 1/2 cup boiling water; drizzle half over the ladyfingers. Spread with half of the pudding mixture. Repeat layers with 9 more split ladyfingers. Sprinkle with 1 tablespoon baking cocoa. Refrigerate leftovers.

Vegetable Risotto

PREP: 10 min. **COOK:** 30 min. + standing

 1 cup chopped onion
 2 teaspoons minced garlic
 1/3 cup butter, cubed
 1-1/2 cups uncooked arborio rice
 1 cup white wine
 4 cups chicken broth
 3 cups fresh broccoli florets
 2 cups chopped yellow summer squash
 2 cups frozen peas, thawed
 1 package (10 ounces) frozen cooked winter squash, thawed
 1/2 teaspoon salt
 1/8 teaspoon white pepper

In a Dutch oven, saute onion and garlic in butter for 2-3 minutes or until tender. Add the rice; cook and stir for 1 minute or until rice is glossy and coated with butter. Stir in wine; cook for 2 minutes or until wine is absorbed.

Stir in the remaining ingredients and bring to a boil. Reduce heat; cover and simmer for 20-25 minutes or until rice is tender. Let stand, uncovered, for 10 minutes before serving.

Yield: 6 servings.

Nutritional Analysis: 1-3/4 cups equals 390 calories, 11 g fat (6 g saturated fat), 27 mg cholesterol, 988 mg sodium, 58 g carbohydrate, 7 g fiber, 10 g protein.

Thawing Frozen Peas

The quickest way to thaw frozen peas is to place them in a strainer or colander and pour boiling water over them.

What Is Risotto?

Risotto refers to an Italian cooking technique used for arborio, a native Italian rice. The rice is sauteed in butter, a liquid is added, and then the mixture simmers, resulting in a unique and tasty creamy dish.

Make It **Meatless**

Thai Vegetable Noodles

PREP/TOTAL TIME: 25 min.

2 teaspoons cornstarch
1/2 cup coconut milk
1/2 cup reduced-sodium soy sauce
1/4 cup water
1/4 cup creamy peanut butter
2 tablespoons rice wine vinegar
5 teaspoons Thai chili sauce
1 tablespoon minced fresh gingerroot
4 ounces uncooked Asian rice noodles
1 pound fresh asparagus, trimmed
   and cut into 1-inch pieces
2 cups fresh snow peas
1 cup julienned sweet red pepper
1 cup shredded carrots
1 can (8 ounces) sliced water chestnuts, drained
1/4 cup chopped shallots
1 tablespoon sesame oil
1/4 cup chopped dry roasted peanuts

In a small bowl, combine the cornstarch, coconut milk, soy sauce, water, peanut butter, vinegar, chili sauce and ginger until blended; set aside.

Cook noodles according to package directions. Meanwhile, in a large skillet, saute the asparagus, snow peas, red pepper, carrots, water chestnuts and shallots in oil for 5-8 minutes or until crisp-tender.

Stir soy sauce mixture and add to the skillet. Bring to a boil; cook and stir for 2 minutes or until thickened. Drain noodles; add to vegetable mixture and stir to coat. Sprinkle with peanuts.

Yield: 4 servings.

Nutritional Analysis: 1-1/4 cups equals 468 calories, 22 g fat (8 g saturated fat), 0 cholesterol, 1,503 mg sodium, 57 g carbohydrate, 8 g fiber, 15 g protein.

Bell Pepper Basics

Look for firm, glossy, bright-colored bell peppers that are unblemished and have smooth skins. Store unwashed bell peppers in the refrigerator crisper drawer for up to 1 week. One pound peppers yields about 4 cups thinly sliced.

Substitution Secret

If you can't find Asian rice noodles in the Oriental cooking section of your grocery store, angel hair pasta or vermicelli can be used in their place.

Roasted Veggie Pasta Salad

PREP: 20 min.　**BAKE:** 30 min.

1　small butternut squash, peeled and cut into 1-inch pieces
2　cups water
1　medium eggplant, cut into 1-inch pieces
1　large zucchini, cut into 1-inch pieces
1　medium sweet red pepper, cut into 1-inch pieces
1　medium red onion, cut into 1-inch pieces
1/2　cup olive oil
1　teaspoon dried marjoram
1　package (16 ounces) tricolor spiral pasta
1/2　cup Italian salad dressing
1/4　cup minced fresh basil
1　teaspoon salt
1/2　teaspoon pepper

Place the squash and water in a microwave-safe bowl. Cover and cook for 10 minutes or until tender; drain.

Arrange the squash, eggplant, zucchini, red pepper and onion in a greased 15-in. x 10-in. x 1-in. baking pan. In a small bowl, whisk the oil and marjoram until combined. Drizzle over vegetables. Bake, uncovered, at 450° for 30 minutes or until tender. Meanwhile, cook pasta according to package directions; drain.

In a large bowl, combine the pasta and roasted vegetables. Stir in the salad dressing, basil, salt and pepper. Serve warm or at room temperature.

Yield: 8 servings.

Nutritional Analysis: 1-3/4 cups equals 461 calories, 20 g fat (3 g saturated fat), 0 cholesterol, 560 mg sodium, 62 g carbohydrate, 8 g fiber, 10 g protein.

Eggplant Primer

Look for eggplant that is firm, pear-shaped and feels heavy for its size. The skin should be smooth and glossy. Avoid eggplant with blemishes or rust spots.

Store unwashed eggplant in the crisper drawer for up to 3 days. Clean just before using; peel if desired.

Time-Saving Tip

You can prepare the pasta in advance and refrigerate it in a resealable plastic bag. When ready to combine with the roasted vegetables, place in a colander and quickly rinse with hot water; drain well.

Pinto Bean Zucchini Boats

PREP/TOTAL TIME: 30 min.

4 large zucchini
8 cups water
1 teaspoon salt
1/2 cup chopped red onion
1 tablespoon olive oil
1 can (16 ounces) pinto beans, rinsed and drained
1 can (11 ounces) Mexicorn, drained
1 can (8 ounces) tomato sauce
1/2 cup chili sauce
1 teaspoon dried cilantro flakes
1/2 teaspoon ground cumin
3 ounces Gouda cheese, shredded
1/2 cup chopped tomato

Cut zucchini in half lengthwise. Scoop out pulp, leaving a 3/8-in. shell. Chop pulp and set aside. In a Dutch oven, bring water and salt to a boil. Add zucchini shells; cook for 5-8 minutes or until crisp-tender. Drain and set aside.

In a large skillet, saute the onion and zucchini pulp in oil until crisp-tender. Stir in the beans, corn, tomato sauce, chili sauce, cilantro and cumin. Cook over medium heat for 5 minutes or until heated through. Sprinkle with cheese; cover and cook for 1 minute or until cheese is melted. Spoon into zucchini shells; sprinkle with tomato.

Yield: 4 servings.

Nutritional Analysis: 2 stuffed zucchini halves equal 368 calories, 10 g fat (4 g saturated fat), 24 mg cholesterol, 2,079 mg sodium, 56 g carbohydrate, 12 g fiber, 18 g protein.

Gouda Cheese Tips

Gouda is a firm smooth Dutch cheese made from cow's milk. It has a mellow, rich caramel flavor. When aged, Gouda is lightly sweet and sharp.

The red wax covering on Gouda cheese helps retain moisture and flavor. Keep the wax coating on any used portions of cheese. Refrigerate leftover cheese in a heavy-duty resealable plastic bag.

Tomato Mac 'n' Cheese

PREP/TOTAL TIME: 30 min.

- 1 package (12 ounces) uncooked penne *or* medium tube pasta
- 3 tablespoons butter
- 3 tablespoons all-purpose flour
- 3 cups milk
- 1 pound white cheddar cheese, shredded
- 1/2 teaspoon salt
- 1/2 teaspoon ground mustard
- 1/4 teaspoon white pepper
- 1 cup chopped seeded tomatoes

Cook pasta according to package directions. Meanwhile, in a Dutch oven, melt butter over medium heat. Stir in flour until smooth; gradually add the milk. Bring to a boil; cook and stir for 2 minutes or until thickened.

Reduce heat to medium. Stir in the cheese, salt, mustard and pepper. Cook and stir until cheese is melted. Drain pasta; stir into cheese sauce. Cook and stir for 3 minutes or until heated through. Stir in tomatoes just until combined.

Yield: 6 servings.

Nutritional Analysis: 1-1/2 cups equals 655 calories, 36 g fat (22 g saturated fat), 111 mg cholesterol, 789 mg sodium, 52 g carbohydrate, 2 g fiber, 31 g protein.

Simple Green Salad

A side salad is all you need to make Tomato Mac 'n' Cheese a real meal.

Start with one 8-ounce package field greens salad blend. Toss in 1-1/2 cups cubed mozzarella, 1/2 cup sliced ripe olives, 2 chopped tomatoes and 1/4 cup pine nuts. Top with 1/2 cup balsamic vinaigrette salad dressing; toss to coat.

Refried Bean Tostadas

PREP/TOTAL TIME: 30 min.

6	flour tortillas (8 inches)
1/2	pound sliced fresh mushrooms
1	cup diced zucchini
2	tablespoons vegetable oil
1	jar (16 ounces) chunky salsa
1	can (11 ounces) shoepeg corn, drained
1	can (16 ounces) vegetarian refried beans, warmed
1-1/2	cups shredded lettuce
1-1/2	cups (6 ounces) shredded cheddar cheese
2	medium ripe avocados, peeled and sliced
1-1/2	cups chopped tomatoes
6	tablespoons sour cream

In a large ungreased skillet, cook tortillas for 1-2 minutes on each side or until lightly browned. Remove and set aside.

In the same skillet, saute mushrooms and zucchini in oil until crisp-tender. Add salsa and corn; cook for 2-3 minutes or until heated through.

Spread refried beans over each tortilla; top with lettuce, salsa mixture, cheese, avocados, tomatoes and sour cream.

Yield: 6 servings.

Nutritional Analysis: 1 serving equals 588 calories, 31 g fat (10 g saturated fat), 40 mg cholesterol, 1,250 mg sodium, 65 g carbohydrate, 15 g fiber, 24 g protein.

Seeding and Slicing Avocados

First cut the avocado lengthwise all the way around, then gently twist the halves in opposite directions to separate them. Firmly—and carefully—hit the seed with the blade of a sharp knife. Twist the knife slightly and lift the seed.

Place half of the avocado cut side up on a cutting board. Cut slices just to but not through the skin. Peel the skin back and remove the slices.

Substitution Secrets

Instead of using flour tortillas, pick up a pack of tostada shells. Or turn this dish into a hearty salad by tossing in more lettuce and using store-bought taco salad shells.

Oven Pancake with Veggies

PREP: 15 min.   **BAKE:** 20 min.

      1   teaspoon butter
    1/2   cup all-purpose flour
      2   eggs, beaten
    1/2   cup milk
    1/2   teaspoon salt, *divided*
      2   cups fresh broccoli florets
      1   cup chopped green pepper
      1   cup chopped tomato
    1/2   cup chopped red onion
      2   tablespoons water
    1/8   teaspoon pepper
  1-1/2   cups (6 ounces) shredded cheddar cheese

Place butter in a 9-in. pie plate; heat in a 450° oven until melted. Carefully tilt pan to coat bottom and sides. In a bowl, beat the flour, eggs, milk and 1/4 teaspoon salt until smooth. Pour into pie plate. Bake for 14-16 minutes or until puffed around the edges and golden brown.

Meanwhile, in a skillet, cook the broccoli, green pepper, tomato and onion in water for 8-10 minutes or until crisp-tender; drain well. Add pepper and remaining salt.

Sprinkle 1/2 cup cheese over pancake; top with vegetables and remaining cheese. Bake 3-4 minutes longer or until cheese is melted. Cut into four wedges; serve immediately.

Yield: 4 servings.

Nutritional Analysis: 1 wedge equals 308 calories, 17 g fat (11 g saturated fat), 158 mg cholesterol, 621 mg sodium, 23 g carbohydrate, 3 g fiber, 17 g protein.

A Sweet Pancake With Pizzazz

For a sweet version of this recipe that would be great for breakfast, prepare the pancake as directed.

Meanwhile, slice 3 apples and 3 pears. Melt 3 tablespoons butter in a large skillet. Cook apple and pear slices and 3 tablespoons sugar for 12-15 minutes or until fruit is tender, stirring occasionally. Pour over pancake.

Make It **Meatless**

Three-Bean Chili

PREP: 10 min. **COOK:** 45 min.

1/2	cup chopped onion
1/2	cup chopped green pepper
1/2	cup chopped celery
1	teaspoon minced garlic
1	tablespoon olive oil
1	can (28 ounces) crushed tomatoes
1	can (14-1/2 ounces) Mexican diced tomatoes
1/4	cup chopped sun-dried tomatoes (not packed in oil)
1	can (16 ounces) pinto beans, rinsed and drained
1	can (16 ounces) kidney beans, rinsed and drained
1	can (15 ounces) black beans, rinsed and drained
1/2	cup dark beer
1	tablespoon chili powder
2	teaspoons baking cocoa
1	cup (4 ounces) shredded Mexican cheese blend

In a Dutch oven, saute the onion, green pepper, celery and garlic in oil until crisp-tender. Add the tomatoes, beans, beer, chili powder and cocoa. Bring to a boil. Reduce heat; cover and simmer for 40 minutes. Serve with cheese.

Yield: 6 servings.

Nutritional Analysis: 1-1/2 cups equals 373 calories, 9 g fat (4 g saturated fat), 17 mg cholesterol, 992 mg sodium, 54 g carbohydrate, 14 g fiber, 19 g protein.

Jazzed-Up Corn Bread

Jazz up ordinary corn bread to serve alongside Three-Bean Chili. Fix one package (8-1/2 ounces) corn bread/muffin mix according to package directions. Stir in 1/2 cup shredded cheddar cheese and one can (8-3/4 ounces) cream-style corn. Bake according to package directions.

Preparation Pointer

On a chilly Saturday afternoon, make a double batch of Three-Bean Chili. Enjoy half for dinner that night, then freeze the rest for a weeknight meal later on.

Cast aside everyday dinners
and net some compliments with
an assortment of
from-the-sea favorites!

Cornmeal-Crusted
Catfish (p. 230)

Fast Fish & Seafood

Crab Couscous Salad

PREP/TOTAL TIME: 30 min.

  2 **cups vegetable broth**
  1 **tablespoon butter**
  1 **package (8 ounces) couscous**
  6 **tablespoons olive oil**
1/4 **cup lemon juice**
1/4 **teaspoon ground cumin**
1-1/2 **pounds imitation crabmeat, coarsely chopped**
1-1/2 **cups chopped peeled mangoes**
  1 **cup quartered cherry tomatoes**
1/4 **cup chopped green onions**

In a saucepan, bring the broth and butter to a boil. Stir in the couscous. Remove from the heat; cover and let stand for 5 minutes. Transfer to a large bowl; cool to room temperature. Fluff with a fork.

For dressing, in a small bowl, combine the oil, lemon juice and cumin. Add the crab, mangoes, tomatoes and onions to couscous. Drizzle with dressing and toss to coat.

Yield: 6 servings.

Nutritional Analysis: 1-1/2 cups equals 443 calories, 17 g fat (3 g saturated fat), 61 mg cholesterol, 429 mg sodium, 53 g carbohydrate, 3 g fiber, 22 g protein.

Lively Leftover

One 14-1/2-ounce can of vegetable broth equals about 1-3/4 cups, so you'll need two cans for this recipe.

Refrigerate or freeze leftover broth and use to make Italian Stew (page 12) or Mushroom Hunter's Sauce (page 192).

Substitution Secret

One cup of bite-size grape tomatoes is a great substitute for the quartered cherry tomatoes in this recipe. There's no need to cut them before tossing into the salad.

Fast **Fish & Seafood**

Salsa Fish

PREP/TOTAL TIME: 20 min.

    2   pounds walleye, bass *or* perch fillets
    1   cup seasoned bread crumbs
    1   tablespoon vegetable oil
1-1/2 cups salsa
    2   cups (8 ounces) shredded mozzarella cheese

Coat fillets with bread crumbs. In a large skillet, brown fillets on both sides in oil. Transfer to a greased 13-in. x 9-in. x 2-in. baking dish. Top with salsa and cheese. Bake, uncovered, at 400° for 7-10 minutes or until fish flakes easily with a fork and cheese is melted.

Yield: 6 servings.

Nutritional Analysis: 1 serving equals 360 calories, 13 g fat (6 g saturated fat), 160 mg cholesterol, 785 mg sodium, 20 g carbohydrate, 5 g fiber, 43 g protein.

Substitution Secret

To give this fish an Italian twist, substitute spaghetti sauce for the salsa. Then serve the saucy fish over buttered noodles.

Testing Fish for Doneness

To test fish for doneness, gently insert the tines of a fork into the thickest part of the fish and wiggle the fork slightly.

When the fish is done, it will flake easily and the flesh will look evenly white and opaque with no more translucent quality.

Pineapple Cabbage Saute (p. 262)

Pecan-Coated Roughy

PREP/TOTAL TIME: 30 min.

1   egg, lightly beaten
3/4   cup finely chopped pecans
4   orange roughy fillets (6 ounces *each*)
1   tablespoon chopped shallot
2   teaspoons butter
1/2   cup white wine
2   teaspoons cornstarch
1   cup orange juice
2   teaspoons Dijon mustard

Place the egg and pecans in separate shallow bowls. Dip fillets into egg, then coat with pecans. Place in a greased 15-in. x 10-in. x 1-in. baking pan. Bake, uncovered, at 400° for 20-25 minutes or until fish flakes easily with a fork.

Meanwhile, in a small saucepan, saute shallot in butter until tender. Add wine. Bring to a boil; cook for 1-2 minutes or until liquid is reduced by half. In a small bowl, combine the cornstarch, orange juice and mustard until smooth; stir into wine mixture. Bring to a boil; cook and stir for 2 minutes or until thickened. Serve with orange roughy.

Yield: 4 servings.

Nutritional Analysis: 1 fillet with 3 tablespoons sauce equals 364 calories, 21 g fat (3 g saturated fat), 92 mg cholesterol, 207 mg sodium, 12 g carbohydrate, 2 g fiber, 29 g protein.

Orange Roughy Facts

Orange roughy is an all-purpose white-fleshed fish. The meat is firm, low in fat and mild in flavor. Any whitefish fillets (like ocean perch, cod, haddock, pollock and red snapper) can be substituted for orange roughy in recipes.

Prepare Some Snow Peas

Before using snow peas, rinse and trim the stem end. Remove the string from the end if desired. One pound of sugar snap peas equals 4 cups and serves 4 to 6 people.

To boil snow peas, place snow peas in a saucepan; add 1 in. of water. Bring to a boil. Reduce heat; cover and simmer for 2-3 minutes or until tender and bright green. Snow peas can also be stir-fried in hot oil for 2-3 minutes.

Citrus Garlic Shrimp

PREP/TOTAL TIME: 25 min.

1 package (1 pound) linguine
1/2 cup olive oil
1/2 cup orange juice
1/3 cup lemon juice
3 to 4 garlic cloves, peeled
5 teaspoons grated lemon peel
4 teaspoons grated orange peel
1 teaspoon salt
1/4 teaspoon pepper
1 pound uncooked medium shrimp, peeled and deveined
Shredded Parmesan cheese and minced fresh parsley, optional

Cook linguine according to package directions. Meanwhile, in a blender or food processor, combine the next eight ingredients; cover and process until blended. Pour into a large skillet; heat through. Add the shrimp; cook for 5 minutes or until shrimp turn pink. Drain linguine; toss with shrimp mixture. Sprinkle with Parmesan cheese and parsley if desired.

Yield: 6 servings.

Nutritional Analysis: 1 cup equals 504 calories, 20 g fat (3 g saturated fat), 112 mg cholesterol, 526 mg sodium, 60 g carbohydrate, 3 g fiber, 22 g protein.

Time-Saving Tips

Whip up the citrus sauce for this recipe earlier in the day or even the night before. Transfer to a covered container; chill.

You can also peel and devein the shrimp ahead of time. Place in a resealable plastic bag and refrigerate. Or pick up some peeled and deveined shrimp from the supermarket.

Scallops Au Gratin

PREP/TOTAL TIME: 30 min.

3   tablespoons all-purpose flour
1   cup milk
1/2   cup heavy whipping cream
1/4   cup white wine
1   teaspoon Dijon mustard
1/4   teaspoon salt
1/4   teaspoon pepper
1-1/2 pounds bay scallops
1/2   cup chopped onion
2   tablespoons butter
1   jar (4-1/2 ounces) sliced mushrooms, drained
1/2   teaspoon dried tarragon
1-1/4 cups shredded Asiago cheese
TOPPING:
1/3   cup dry bread crumbs
2   tablespoons butter, melted
1   tablespoon grated Parmesan cheese

In a bowl, combine the flour, milk, cream, wine, mustard, salt and pepper until smooth; set aside. In a large skillet, saute scallops and onion in butter until scallops are opaque. Remove with a slotted spoon. Add milk mixture to the skillet. Bring to a boil; cook and stir for 2 minutes or until thickened.

Drain scallops. Add the scallops, mushrooms and tarragon to the sauce; heat through. Stir in Asiago cheese until melted.

Divide scallop mixture among four 10-oz. baking dishes. Combine the topping ingredients; sprinkle over scallop mixture. Broil 6 in. from the heat for 1-2 minutes or until golden brown.

Yield: 4 servings.

Nutritional Analysis: 1 cup equals 534 calories, 31 g fat (18 g saturated fat), 150 mg cholesterol, 885 mg sodium, 23 g carbohydrate, 2 g fiber, 39 g protein.

Preparation Pointer

Cooked scallops will continue to release juices. To create a thick sauce, it's important to drain the liquid before returning the scallops to the pan.

Selecting Scallops

There are many varieties of scallops, from tiny, tender bay scallops to large, less-tender sea scallops.

Overcooking scallops makes them tough and rubbery. It's best to cook them quickly by sauteing, grilling, broiling or poaching.

Fast **Fish & Seafood**

Tomato 'n' Shrimp Pasta

PREP/TOTAL TIME: 30 min.

12	ounces uncooked spaghetti
1-1/2	pounds uncooked medium shrimp, peeled and deveined
1	teaspoon minced garlic
3	tablespoons olive oil, *divided*
1/2	pound sliced fresh mushrooms
1/2	cup chopped onion
2	cans (14-1/2 ounces *each*) diced tomatoes, undrained
3	tablespoons tomato paste
2	tablespoons minced fresh basil
1	teaspoon sugar
1	teaspoon dried oregano
1/4	to 1/2 teaspoon crushed red pepper flakes

Cook spaghetti according to package directions. Meanwhile, in a large skillet, saute shrimp and garlic in 1 tablespoon oil until shrimp turn pink. Remove and set aside.

In the same skillet, saute mushrooms and onion in remaining oil until mushrooms are lightly browned. Stir in the tomatoes and tomato paste. Bring to a boil. Reduce heat to low. Add the shrimp, basil, sugar, oregano and red pepper flakes. Cook, uncovered, for 5-10 minutes or until heated through. Drain spaghetti; top with shrimp mixture.

Yield: 6 servings.

Nutritional Analysis: 1 serving equals 410 calories, 9 g fat (1 g saturated fat), 168 mg cholesterol, 379 mg sodium, 54 g carbohydrate, 5 g fiber, 28 g protein.

Freezing Tomato Paste

Oftentimes, a recipe calls for a tablespoon or two of tomato paste. Measure left-over tomato paste into 1-tablespoon servings and place in an ice cube tray. Cover and freeze overnight. Transfer to a resealable plastic bag and freeze for future use.

Peeling and Deveining Shrimp

Remove the shell from the raw shrimp by opening the shell at the underside of leg area and peeling it back. To remove the black vein, make a slit with a paring knife along the back from the head area to the tail. Rinse under cold water to remove the exposed vein.

Fish Po'Boys

PREP/TOTAL TIME: 30 min.

- 2 packages (11.4 ounces *each*) frozen crunchy breaded fish fillets
- 1/2 cup mayonnaise
- 1 tablespoon minced fresh parsley
- 1 tablespoon ketchup
- 2 teaspoons stone-ground mustard
- 1 teaspoon horseradish sauce
- 2 to 4 drops hot pepper sauce
- 1-1/2 cups deli coleslaw
- 6 hamburger buns, split

Bake fish according to package directions. Meanwhile, in a small bowl, combine the mayonnaise, parsley, ketchup, mustard, horseradish sauce and hot pepper sauce until blended. Spoon 1/4 cup coleslaw onto the bottom of each bun; top with two pieces of fish. Spread with sauce; replace bun tops.

Yield: 6 servings.

Nutritional Analysis: 1 sandwich with 2 tablespoons sauce equals 588 calories, 36 g fat (6 g saturated fat), 39 mg cholesterol, 1,165 mg sodium, 52 g carbohydrate, 4 g fiber, 14 g protein.

Preparation Pointer

Although we used a garlic and herb variety of frozen fish to make these sandwiches, feel free to use your favorite flavor. Ideas include lemon-pepper, ranch or Parmesan.

If you decide to go with beer battered fish, you may want to use onion rolls in place of ordinary hamburger buns to add a little more flavor.

Salmon Patties with Caper Mayonnaise

PREP/TOTAL TIME: 30 min.

  6   **tablespoons mayonnaise**
  2   **teaspoons capers, drained**
  2   **to 3 teaspoons lemon juice**
3-1/2 **teaspoons Dijon mustard,** *divided*
  1/2 **teaspoon pepper,** *divided*
  1/4 **cup finely chopped onion**
  1/4 **cup finely chopped celery**
  5   **teaspoons vegetable oil,** *divided*
  2   **cans (6 ounces** *each***) skinless boneless salmon, drained**
  3/4 **cup seasoned bread crumbs,** *divided*
  1   **egg, lightly beaten**

In a small bowl, combine the mayonnaise, capers, lemon juice, 1/2 teaspoon mustard and 1/4 teaspoon pepper. Cover and refrigerate until serving.

In a small skillet, saute the onion and celery in 1 teaspoon oil until crisp-tender. In a bowl, combine the onion mixture, salmon, 1/2 cup bread crumbs, egg and remaining mustard and pepper. Shape into four patties; coat with remaining bread crumbs. Cover and refrigerate for 10 minutes.

In a large skillet over medium heat, cook salmon patties in remaining oil for 5 minutes on each side or until lightly browned. Serve with caper mayonnaise.

Yield: 2 servings.

Nutritional Analysis: 2 patties with 1/4 cup mayonnaise equals 806 calories, 56 g fat (10 g saturated fat), 181 mg cholesterol, 2,057 mg sodium, 34 g carbohydrate, 2 g fiber, 40 g protein.

Caper Primer

Capers are the dried flower buds of a bush native to the Mediterranean and parts of Asia that are pickled and sold in jars. Because of their intense, distinctive flavor, capers are used in moderate amounts. To remove some of the excess salt from capers, rinse in cold water before using. Look for capers in the condiment aisle of your grocery store.

Cornmeal-Crusted Catfish

PREP/TOTAL TIME: 30 min.

    1   egg, lightly beaten
    2   tablespoons lemon juice
  1/2   cup all-purpose flour
  1/4   cup yellow cornmeal
    1   teaspoon Cajun seasoning
  1/2   teaspoon garlic powder
  1/2   teaspoon salt
    4   catfish fillets (6 ounces *each*)
    3   tablespoons vegetable oil

In a shallow bowl, combine the egg and lemon juice. In another shallow bowl, combine the flour, cornmeal, Cajun seasoning, garlic powder and salt. Dip catfish into egg mixture, then coat with cornmeal mixture.

In a large skillet, heat oil over medium heat. Fry fillets, two at a time, for 5-6 minutes on each side or until fish flakes easily with a fork.

Yield: 4 servings.

Nutritional Analysis: *1 fillet equals 430 calories, 25 g fat (5 g saturated fat), 133 mg cholesterol, 568 mg sodium, 20 g carbohydrate, 1 g fiber, 30 g protein.*

Better Breading

To help the breading adhere to the catfish, first pat the fillets dry and coat lightly with flour. Then dip fish into the beaten egg and dredge in the cornmeal mixture. Let stand for 5-10 minutes before frying.

Speedy Side Dish

Along with a Strawberry Spinach Salad (page 280), Lemon Rice would nicely complement Cornmeal-Crusted Catfish.

In a medium saucepan, bring 1 cup water, 1 cup chicken broth, 2 tablespoons lemon juice and 2 teaspoons butter to a boil. Stir in 1 cup uncooked long grain rice, 1/4 teaspoon dried basil and 1/4 teaspoon grated lemon peel.

Reduce heat; cover and simmer for 20 minutes. Let stand for 5 minutes or until the liquid is absorbed.

Strawberry Spinach Salad (p. 280)

Scallop Pesto Pasta

PREP/TOTAL TIME: 25 min.

8 ounces uncooked angel hair pasta
1/2 cup all-purpose flour
1/2 teaspoon salt
1/4 teaspoon pepper
1 pound sea scallops
3 tablespoons butter
1/2 cup prepared pesto

Cook pasta according to package directions. Meanwhile, in a large resealable plastic bag, combine the flour, salt and pepper; add scallops and shake to coat.

In a large skillet, cook scallops in butter for 2-1/2 to 3 minutes on each side or until opaque. Drain pasta; toss with pesto. Top with scallops.

Yield: 4 servings.

Nutritional Analysis: 1 serving equals 598 calories, 25 g fat (9 g saturated fat), 70 mg cholesterol, 807 mg sodium, 59 g carbohydrate, 3 g fiber, 34 g protein.

Pasta Pointers

Adding oil to the water does not prevent pasta from sticking or boiling over. Instead, the oil coats the cooked pasta and prevents the sauce from sticking.

Stir noodles within the first minute after adding to the boiling water to prevent sticking and keep the water at a full rolling boil. Cook just until "al dente" or firm yet tender. Immediately drain, shake to remove excess water and toss with the sauce while still hot.

Super Sea Scallops

Sea scallops can range from 1/2 to 1 inch thick. To cook thicker scallops more quickly, cut them in half horizontally.

Salmon Quesadillas

PREP/TOTAL TIME: 15 min.

1   teaspoon minced garlic
1   teaspoon vegetable oil
1   can (14-3/4 ounces) salmon, drained, bones and skin removed
1   to 2 teaspoons dried basil
1/2   teaspoon pepper
1   tablespoon butter, softened
4   flour tortillas (8 inches)
2   cups (8 ounces) shredded mozzarella cheese

In a skillet, saute garlic in oil until tender. Stir in the salmon, basil and pepper. Cook over medium heat until heated through.

Spread butter over one side of each tortilla; place buttered side down on a griddle. Sprinkle 1/4 cup cheese over half of each tortilla; top with salmon mixture and remaining cheese. Fold tortilla over filling. Cook over low heat for 1-2 minutes on each side or until cheese is melted. Cut each into three wedges.

Yield: 4 servings.

Nutritional Analysis: 3 wedges equals 664 calories, 39 g fat (19 g saturated fat), 142 mg cholesterol, 1,264 mg sodium, 29 g carbohydrate, trace fiber, 48 g protein.

Keep Canned Salmon on Hand

Sockeye is the preferred type of salmon for canning due to its firm colorful flesh. Cans of salmon can remain in your pantry for 1 year.

Once opened, canned salmon should be transferred to an airtight container, refrigerated and eaten within 3 days. Canned salmon can also be frozen in a tightly-sealed container for up to 3 months.

Simple Salad Dressing

It's easy to encourage your family to eat salads and vegetables when they're topped with an irresistible homemade dressing!

In a jar with a tight-fitting lid, combine 1/3 cup apricot nectar, 1/3 cup red wine vinegar, 1/3 cup canola oil, 1 tablespoon minced fresh parsley, 2 teaspoons Dijon mustard, 1/4 teaspoon salt and 1/8 teaspoon pepper. Shake until blended. Store in the refrigerator.

Tuna with Wasabi Sauce

PREP: 5 min. + marinating   **GRILL:** 10 min.

- 1/4   cup reduced-sodium teriyaki sauce
-   1   tablespoon rice wine vinegar
-   2   teaspoons sesame oil
-   4   tuna steaks (8 ounces *each*)
- 1/2   cup wasabi horseradish mayonnaise
-   2   tablespoons chopped green onion
-   2   teaspoons lemon juice

In a large resealable plastic bag, combine the teriyaki sauce, vinegar and oil; add tuna. Seal bag and turn to coat; refrigerate for up to 1 hour. Meanwhile, in a small bowl, combine the mayonnaise, onion and lemon juice until blended. Refrigerate until serving.

Coat grill rack with nonstick cooking spray before starting the grill. Drain and discard marinade. Grill tuna, uncovered, over medium heat for 5-6 minutes on each side or until fish flakes easily with a fork. Serve with wasabi sauce.

Yield: 4 servings.

Nutritional Analysis: 1 tuna steak with about 2 tablespoons sauce equals 458 calories, 25 g fat (4 g saturated fat), 112 mg cholesterol, 341 mg sodium, 1 g carbohydrate, trace fiber, 53 g protein.

Where to Find Wasabi

Wasabi horseradish mayonnaise can be found in the Asian section of your local supermarket.

Wasabi, an Asian plant similar to horseradish, has a fiery flavor. If it's too spicy for your family's taste, stir in some plain mayonnaise to make a milder sauce.

Crab Chowder

PREP/TOTAL TIME: 25 min.

1/2   pound sliced fresh mushrooms
1/2   cup chopped celery
1/2   cup chopped onion
1/4   cup butter, cubed
1/4   cup all-purpose flour
  2   cups milk
  2   cans (6 ounces *each*) crabmeat,
      drained, flaked and cartilage
      removed
  1   can (14-1/2 ounces) vegetable
      broth
  1   can (14-1/2 ounces) whole potatoes, drained and
      cut into 1/2-inch cubes
  1   cup frozen corn, thawed
  1   teaspoon salt
1/2   teaspoon dill weed
1/2   teaspoon pepper
  2   tablespoons sherry

In a Dutch oven, saute the mushrooms, celery and onion in butter until tender. Stir in flour until blended; gradually add milk. Bring to a boil; cook and stir for 2 minutes or until thickened.

Add the crab, broth, potatoes, corn, salt, dill and pepper. Reduce heat; cover and simmer for 10 minutes or until heated through. Stir in sherry.

Yield: 6 servings.

Nutritional Analysis: 1-1/4 cups equals 272 calories, 12 g fat (7 g saturated fat), 82 mg cholesterol, 1,151 mg sodium, 24 g carbohydrate, 3 g fiber, 19 g protein.

Canned Crab Facts

Taste canned crabmeat before using. If it has a metallic flavor, let it soak in ice water for 5 minutes; drain and blot dry.

Use your fingers to remove the cartilage and any small pieces of shell. Once you open a can of crabmeat, refrigerate it and use within 2 days.

Substitution Secret

For a thicker, heartier chowder, use heavy whipping cream or half-and-half instead of milk.

Vegetable Crab Soup

PREP/TOTAL TIME: 20 min.

    1   can (19 ounces) ready-to-serve clam chowder
    1   can (11 ounces) condensed cheddar cheese soup,
         undiluted
2-1/2   to 3 cups half-and-half cream, *divided*
  1/4   cup white wine
    1   tablespoon Worcestershire sauce
    1   package (16 ounces) frozen stir-fry vegetable
         blend
    2   cans (6 ounces *each*) crabmeat, drained, flaked
         and cartilage removed
    1   medium tomato, seeded and chopped
  2/3   cup shredded cheddar cheese
    2   tablespoons minced fresh parsley
  1/4   to 1/2 teaspoon pepper

In a large saucepan, combine the chowder, soup, 2-1/2 cups cream, wine and Worcestershire sauce. Bring to a boil. Stir in vegetables; return to a boil. Reduce heat; cover and simmer for 6-8 minutes or until vegetables are crisp-tender.

Stir in the crab, tomato, cheese, parsley and pepper. Cook and stir until heated through, adding remaining cream if desired.

Yield: 8 servings.

Nutritional Analysis: 1 cup equals 314 calories, 17 g fat (9 g saturated fat), 93 mg cholesterol, 844 mg sodium, 20 g carbohydrate, 3 g fiber, 18 g protein.

Mincing Fresh Parsley

In many cases (like the recipe here), the amount of parsley added doesn't need to be exact. Skip the cutting board, knife and measuring spoon and simply mince with a kitchen shears directly into the prepared dish.

Speedy Side Dish

Supermarkets offer a variety of fresh breads, from the ever-popular French, Italian and sourdough to an assortment of flavored varieties. Pick up a loaf to serve with this soup.

Creamy Swordfish on Noodles

PREP/TOTAL TIME: 20 min.

4   cups uncooked egg noodles
1   pound swordfish steak, cut into 1/2-inch cubes
1   teaspoon salt, *divided*
1/2 teaspoon pepper, *divided*
1   tablespoon olive oil
1   tablespoon all-purpose flour
1   cup heavy whipping cream
1   cup (4 ounces) shredded mozzarella cheese
1   cup (4 ounces) shredded Parmesan cheese
1   package (16 ounces) frozen California-blend vegetables, thawed

Cook noodles according to package directions. Meanwhile, sprinkle swordfish with 1/2 teaspoon salt and 1/4 teaspoon pepper. In a large skillet, saute swordfish in oil for 5-6 minutes or until opaque. Using a slotted spoon, transfer to a bowl; keep warm.

In a small bowl, combine flour and cream until smooth; add to the skillet. Stir in the cheeses. Bring to a boil; cook and stir for 2 minutes or until thickened. Stir in the fish, vegetables and remaining salt and pepper. Cook for 5 minutes or until heated through. Drain noodles; top with swordfish mixture.

Yield: 4 servings.

Nutritional Analysis: 1 cup swordfish mixture with 1 cup noodles equal 711 calories, 43 g fat (23 g saturated fat), 195 mg cholesterol, 1,200 mg sodium, 37 g carbohydrate, 4 g fiber, 43 g protein.

Swordfish Facts

Swordfish has a firm, meaty texture, making it great for stir-fries and kabobs. It's sold either as fillets or already cubed.

The color of swordfish naturally varies, depending on their diet. On the East Coast, swordfish flesh is pinkish, while California swordfish is creamy white.

Regardless of the color, the flesh should be slightly translucent and have a bright sheen. The lighter flesh should never be gray, and the darker flesh should be reddish to reddish-brown. Darker brown coloration hints of old age.

Tuna, grouper and shark can be substituted for swordfish.

Catfish in Ginger Sauce

PREP/TOTAL TIME: 15 min.

1/2 cup chopped green onions
  1 tablespoon vegetable oil
1/4 teaspoon ground ginger
  1 teaspoon cornstarch
  2 tablespoons water
  1 cup chicken broth
  1 tablespoon soy sauce
  1 tablespoon white wine vinegar
1/8 teaspoon cayenne pepper
  4 catfish fillets (6 ounces *each*)

In a 2-cup microwave-safe bowl, combine the onions, oil and ginger. Microwave, uncovered, on high for 1-1/2 minutes or until onions are tender.

In small bowl, combine the cornstarch and water until smooth. Stir in the broth, soy sauce, vinegar and cayenne. Stir into onion mixture. Microwave, uncovered, at 70% power for 2-3 minutes, stirring after each minute, until sauce comes to a boil.

Place catfish in a microwave-safe 3-qt. dish; pour sauce over the fish. Cover and microwave on high for 5-6 minutes or until fish flakes easily with a fork.

Editor's Note: This recipe was tested in a 1,100-watt microwave.

Yield: 4 servings.

Nutritional Analysis: 1 serving equals 274 calories, 16 g fat (3 g saturated fat), 80 mg cholesterol, 555 mg sodium, 2 g carbohydrate, trace fiber, 28 g protein.

Fresh Versus Dried Herbs

Fresh herbs give foods fabulous flavor. The general ratio to substitute fresh herbs for dried is 3 to 1. That is, use 3 times as much fresh herbs as dried herbs.

For gingerroot, the ratio is 4 to 1. So in this recipe, use 1 teaspoon of fresh grated gingerroot for the ground ginger.

Baked Spiced Salmon

PREP/TOTAL TIME: 30 min.

- 4 salmon fillets (6 ounces *each*)
- 3 tablespoons lime juice, *divided*
- 1/2 teaspoon salt
- 1/2 teaspoon ground ginger
- 1/2 teaspoon ground coriander
- 1/4 teaspoon ground cumin
- 1/8 teaspoon ground cinnamon
- 1/8 teaspoon cayenne pepper
- 1 carton (6 ounces) plain yogurt
- 3 green onions, sliced
- 2 tablespoons minced fresh cilantro

Place the salmon in a greased 13-in. x 9-in. x 2-in. baking dish. Drizzle with 2 tablespoons lime juice. Combine the salt, ginger, coriander, cumin, cinnamon and cayenne; sprinkle over salmon.

Bake, uncovered, at 425° for 18-22 minutes or until fish flakes easily with a fork. Meanwhile, in a small bowl, combine the yogurt, onions, cilantro and remaining lime juice. Serve with salmon.

Yield: 4 servings.

Nutritional Analysis: 1 fillet with about 4-1/2 teaspoons sauce equals 347 calories, 20 g fat (5 g saturated fat), 106 mg cholesterol, 417 mg sodium, 4 g carbohydrate, 1 g fiber, 36 g protein.

Speedy Side Dish

If your family won't care for the Brussels Sprouts with Pecans (page 272) shown with this salmon, here's another idea.

Cut 1 medium zucchini and 1 medium yellow summer squash into 1/4-in. slices. Julienne 1 medium sweet red, orange or yellow pepper. In a skillet, saute vegetables in 1 tablespoon olive oil for 6-8 minutes or until crisp-tender. Sprinkle with 1/2 cup seasoned bread crumbs and 1-1/2 teaspoons dried basil.

Brussels Sprouts with Pecans (p. 272)

244

Shrimp Jambalaya

PREP: 15 min.　　**COOK:** 30 min.

1	cup chopped onion
1/2	cup chopped celery
1/2	cup chopped green pepper
1/4	cup butter, cubed
3	cups vegetable broth
1-1/2	cups uncooked long grain rice
2	teaspoons Creole seasoning
1/2	teaspoon Worcestershire sauce
1/8 to 1/4	teaspoon cayenne pepper
2	cans (14-1/2 ounces *each*) diced tomatoes, drained
1	pound cooked medium shrimp, peeled and deveined
1-1/2	cups frozen peas

In a large skillet, saute the onion, celery and green pepper in butter until tender. Add the broth, rice, Creole seasoning, Worcestershire sauce and cayenne. Bring to a boil. Reduce heat to low; cover and cook for 15-20 minutes or until rice is tender. Stir in the tomatoes, shrimp and peas; heat through.

Yield: 6 servings.

Nutritional Analysis: 1-1/2 cups equals 397 calories, 10 g fat (5 g saturated fat), 135 mg cholesterol, 1,141 mg sodium, 54 g carbohydrate, 5 g fiber, 23 g protein.

Cooking Shrimp

To cook raw shrimp, add 1 pound shrimp and 1 teaspoon salt to 3 quarts boiling water. Reduce heat and simmer, uncovered, for 1-3 minutes or until the shrimp turns pink and curls. Watch closely to avoid overcooking. Drain immediately.

Or pick up 12 to 13 ounces of cooked, peeled and deveined shrimp for this recipe at the grocery store.

Spicy Seasonings

Spice up this shrimp and rice dish to your taste by increasing the amount of Creole seasoning and cayenne pepper. Also add a few drops of hot pepper sauce if desired.

Halibut Provencale

PREP: 10 min.   **BAKE:** 30 min.

4 halibut steaks (6 ounces *each*)
1 cup white wine
1-1/2 cups chopped plum tomatoes
1/4 cup chopped onion
2 tablespoons minced fresh basil
2 tablespoons minced fresh parsley
2 tablespoons chopped ripe olives
1 teaspoon minced garlic
1/4 teaspoon pepper
1/3 cup dry bread crumbs
2 tablespoons butter, melted
1 tablespoon grated Parmesan cheese

Place the halibut in a greased 13-in. x 9-in. x 2-in. baking dish. Pour wine into dish. Combine the tomatoes, onion, basil, parsley, olives, garlic and pepper; spoon over fish. Bake, uncovered, at 350° for 30-35 minutes or until fish flakes easily with a fork.

Combine the bread crumbs, butter and Parmesan cheese; sprinkle over tomato mixture. Broil 3-4 in. from the heat for 1 minute or until golden brown.

Yield: 4 servings.

Nutritional Analysis: 1 serving equals 349 calories, 11 g fat (5 g saturated fat), 71 mg cholesterol, 309 mg sodium, 13 g carbohydrate, 2 g fiber, 38 g protein.

The Basics of Halibut

Halibut is a firm, fine-textured fish with a delicate flavor that can be somewhat dry. (Cooking it in wine in this recipe keeps it moist.)

Look for halibut steaks with pure white flesh and a slightly sweet smell. Steer clear of halibut that is brown or looks dry.

Halibut poaches, grills, broils, braises and steams particularly well. It is also good roasted or sauteed. The edible skin does not need to be removed before cooking. In fact, leaving the skin intact helps the halibut keeps its shape.

Salmon with Fruit Salsa

PREP: 15 min. + standing   **GRILL:** 15 min.

2	cups chopped seedless watermelon
1-1/2	cups cubed fresh pineapple
1/3	cup chopped sweet red pepper
1/4	cup chopped green onions
1/4	cup minced fresh cilantro
1/4	cup orange juice
1/4	cup lime juice
1	teaspoon chopped jalapeno pepper
1/2	teaspoon salt, *divided*
1/4	teaspoon pepper, *divided*
4	salmon fillets (6 ounces *each*)

For salsa, in a large bowl, combine the first eight ingredients; add 1/4 teaspoon salt and 1/8 teaspoon pepper. Let stand at room temperature for at least 30 minutes.

Coat grill rack with nonstick cooking spray before starting the grill. Sprinkle salmon with remaining salt and pepper. Place on grill rack. Grill, covered, over medium heat for 5 minutes. Turn and grill 7-9 minutes longer or until fish flakes easily with a fork. Serve the salsa with a slotted spoon with salmon.

Editor's Note: When cutting or seeding hot peppers, use rubber or plastic gloves to protect your hands. Avoid touching your face.

Yield: 4 servings.

Nutritional Analysis: 1 fillet with 1 cup salsa equals 381 calories, 19 g fat (4 g saturated fat), 100 mg cholesterol, 399 mg sodium, 17 g carbohydrate, 2 g fiber, 35 g protein.

Salmon Savvy

Look for fresh salmon steaks and fillets that are firm with a deep "salmon pink" color. The meat should have a slight sheen and appear somewhat translucent. Choose steaks and fillets with smooth cuts. Cuts of salmon that have gaps are indicative of old fish. Use or freeze fresh salmon within 2 days of purchase.

When buying frozen salmon, look for solidly frozen packages stored below the chill line in the freezer case. Don't buy salmon with freezer burns or icy white discoloration. Use frozen salmon within 3 months.

Round out your weeknight meals with an assortment of garden-fresh veggies, satisfying grains and cool salads.

Grilled Asparagus (p. 259)

Swift Sides & Salads

Wild Rice Salad

PREP: 15 min. + chilling

  2 **cups cooked wild rice**
  1 **cup cherry tomatoes, halved**
1/2 **cup chopped peeled cucumber**
1/2 **cup sliced celery**
1/3 **cup chopped pecans, toasted**
1/4 **cup chopped red onion**
1/2 **teaspoon salt**
1/4 **teaspoon pepper**
1/4 **cup honey mustard salad dressing**

In a large bowl, combine the rice, tomatoes, cucumber, celery, pecans, onion, salt and pepper. Drizzle with dressing and toss to coat. Cover and refrigerate for 30 minutes before serving.

Yield: 6 servings.

Nutritional Analysis: 3/4 cup equals 148 calories, 8 g fat (1 g saturated fat), 0 cholesterol, 280 mg sodium, 17 g carbohydrate, 2 g fiber, 3 g protein.

How to Cook Wild Rice

If you're making wild rice to serve with Turkey Pear Skillet on page 127, make a little extra and refrigerate for this salad the next day.

Here's an easy recipe for cooking wild rice that yields 3 to 4 cups.

Thoroughly wash 1 cup uncooked wild rice. In a large saucepan, bring 3 cups salted water to a boil; stir in rice. Return water to boil and stir. Reduce heat; cover and simmer for 50-60 minutes or just until kernels puff open. Uncover and fluff with a fork. Simmer 5 additional minutes; drain any excess liquid.

For faster preparation, turn to a long grain wild rice mix.

Broiled Tomatoes with Artichokes

PREP/TOTAL TIME: 15 min.

    3   small tomatoes, halved
    1   jar (7-1/2 ounces) marinated artichoke hearts,
        drained and chopped
  1/2   cup crumbled feta cheese
  1/3   cup dry bread crumbs
    2   tablespoons butter, melted

With a sharp knife, remove the seeds and pulp from the center of each tomato half. Place cut side up on a foil-lined baking sheet. Combine the artichokes and cheese; place 2 tablespoons in the center of each tomato. Broil 3-4 in. from the heat for 2-3 minutes or until bubbly.

Toss the bread crumbs and butter; sprinkle over tomatoes. Broil 3-4 in. from the heat for 1-2 minutes or until browned.

Yield: 6 servings.

Nutritional Analysis: 1 tomato half equals 145 calories, 11 g fat (5 g saturated fat), 15 mg cholesterol, 306 mg sodium, 9 g carbohydrate, 1 g fiber, 3 g protein.

Tomato Tips

When looking to buy tomatoes, select those that are brightly colored with a smooth, blemish-free skin. They should be firm and give slightly to pressure.

Keep unwashed tomatoes at room temperature for 1 to 2 days. Refrigerating will reduce some of the flavor.

To ripen tomatoes, place in a brown paper bag with an apple for several days.

Some recipes (like the one here) require you to seed the tomato, which will reduce the amount of juice. (In recipes that are more saucy, the seeds can remain.) To seed a tomato, cut in half and gently squeeze over a bowl. Use a small spoon to remove any seeds or membranes.

Chutney Turkey Salad (p. 130)

Mixed Greens with Goat Cheese

PREP/TOTAL TIME: 20 min.

1/2 cup all-purpose flour
1 cup sliced almonds
1 egg
1 tablespoon water
2 packages (4 ounces *each*) goat cheese
1 package (10 ounces) Italian-blend salad greens
1/3 cup balsamic vinaigrette

Place flour and almonds in separate shallow bowls. In another shallow bowl, beat egg and water. Cut each cheese log into six slices; roll in flour, then dip into egg mixture. Roll in almonds, pressing gently into cheese. Place in a 13-in. x 9-in. x 2-in. baking dish coated with nonstick cooking spray. Bake at 350° for 10 minutes or until lightly browned.

Divide salad greens among six plates; top each with two warm cheese slices. Drizzle with vinaigrette.

Yield: 6 servings.

Nutritional Analysis: 1 serving equals 210 calories, 11 g fat (1 g saturated fat), 35 mg cholesterol, 128 mg sodium, 14 g carbohydrate, 3 g fiber, 6 g protein.

Get to Know Goat Cheese

The texture of goat cheese can vary from soft (in fresh cheese) to semi-firm (in aged cheese). Look for this cheese in the specialty cheese section of your local grocery store. It comes plain or mixed with herbs and is packed in various shapes and sizes. Fresh goat cheese should look moist. Don't buy it if it's moldy or wet.

In the refrigerator, protect goat cheese from air with original wrappings or plastic wrap. You can also tightly wrap and freeze goat cheese for longer storage. Let it thaw in the refrigerator for 2 to 3 days.

Cranberry Couscous

PREP/TOTAL TIME: 15 min.

    1 **can (14-1/2 ounces) chicken broth**
    1 **tablespoon butter**
1-1/2 **cups uncooked couscous**
  1/4 **cup dried cranberries, chopped**
    3 **tablespoons chopped green onions**

In a small saucepan, bring broth and butter to a boil. Stir in the couscous, cranberries and onions. Remove from the heat. Cover and let stand for 5 minutes or until broth is absorbed. Fluff with a fork.

Yield: 6 servings.

Nutritional Analysis: 3/4 cup equals 202 calories, 3 g fat (1 g saturated fat), 5 mg cholesterol, 295 mg sodium, 39 g carbohydrate, 2 g fiber, 7 g protein.

Crazy About Cranberries

Dried cranberries are a great way to boost the nutrition in foods throughout the day. Sprinkle them on cereal or your favorite salad. Mix some into entrees, muffins and desserts. Eat them out of the bag for a healthy snack.

You can also find flavored dried cranberries. Experiment with them in this side dish for a tasty twist.

Grilled Asparagus

PREP/TOTAL TIME: 20 min.

> 1   cup water
> 1   pound fresh asparagus, trimmed
> 1/4 cup barbecue sauce

In a large skillet, bring water to a boil; add asparagus. Cover and cook for 4-6 minutes or until almost tender; drain and pat dry. Cool slightly.

Thread several asparagus spears onto two parallel soaked wooden skewers. Repeat. Grill, uncovered, over medium heat for 2 minutes, turning once. Baste with barbecue sauce. Grill 2 minutes longer, turning and basting once.

Yield: 4 servings.

Nutritional Analysis: 3 asparagus spears equals 25 calories, trace fat (trace saturated fat), 0 cholesterol, 133 mg sodium, 4 g carbohydrate, 1 g fiber, 2 g protein.

Buying and Storing Asparagus

Look for small, straight asparagus stalks with tightly closed, compact tips. The spears should be smooth and round. The stalks should have a bright green color, while the tips may have a slight lavender tint.

Refrigerate unwashed asparagus in a sealed plastic bag for up to 4 days.

When ready to use, soak asparagus in cold water to clean. Snap off the stalk ends as far down as they will easily break when gently bent.

Broccoli with Red Pepper

PREP/TOTAL TIME: 20 min.

    1   cup chicken broth
    1   pound fresh broccoli spears
    1   cup julienned sweet red pepper
    2   tablespoons chopped shallot
    2   tablespoons olive oil
  1/3   cup slivered almonds
  1/2   teaspoon lemon-pepper seasoning
  1/4   teaspoon salt

In a large saucepan, bring broth to a boil. Cut broccoli spears in half lengthwise; add to broth. Reduce heat; cover and simmer for 5-8 minutes or until crisp-tender.

Meanwhile, in a large skillet, saute red pepper and shallot in oil for 5 minutes or until crisp-tender. Drain broccoli; add broccoli, almonds, lemon-pepper and salt to skillet. Cook and stir for 2 minutes or until broccoli is tender.

Yield: 4 servings.

Nutritional Analysis: 3/4 cup equals 157 calories, 12 g fat (1 g saturated fat), 0 cholesterol, 468 mg sodium, 10 g carbohydrate, 5 g fiber, 6 g protein.

Buying and Storing Broccoli

Select firm yet tender stalks of broccoli with compact, dark green or slightly purplish florets.

Keep unwashed broccoli in an open plastic bag in the refrigerator crisper drawer for up to 4 days.

Before using, remove the large outer leaves and tough ends of the lower stalks. Rinse in cold water. If using whole spears, cut lengthwise into 1-in.-wide pieces. Stalks may also be peeled for more even cooking.

Pineapple Cabbage Saute

PREP/TOTAL TIME: 20 min.

1   **can (8 ounces) crushed pineapple**
6   **cups thinly sliced cabbage**
1   **tablespoon olive oil**
2   **tablespoons honey mustard salad dressing**
1/8 **teaspoon white pepper**

Drain pineapple, reserving 1 tablespoon juice; set aside. In a large skillet, saute cabbage in oil for 5-8 minutes or until crisp-tender. Add the salad dressing, pepper and reserved pineapple and juice. Cook for 1 minute or until heated through.

Yield: 6 servings.

Nutritional Analysis: 3/4 cup equals 85 calories, 4 g fat (1 g saturated fat), 0 cholesterol, 48 mg sodium, 12 g carbohydrate, 2 g fiber, 1 g protein.

The Basics of Buying Cabbage

Buy round, compact solid green heads that seem heavy for their size. The leaves should be tight, smooth and unblemished.

Place unwashed cabbage in a sealed plastic bag in your refrigerator crisper drawer for 1 to 2 weeks.

Wash just before using. Remove any discolored, damaged or tough outer leaves from the head.

Squash Hominy Soup

PREP/TOTAL TIME: 20 min.

2/3 cup chopped onion
1 teaspoon minced garlic
1 tablespoon butter
2 packages (10 ounces *each*) frozen cooked winter squash, thawed
2 cups chicken broth
1 can (15-1/2 ounces) hominy, rinsed and drained
1 teaspoon salt
1/4 teaspoon pepper
1/4 teaspoon *each* ground ginger, cinnamon and nutmeg
1/4 cup heavy whipping cream

In a large saucepan, saute onion and garlic in butter until tender. Stir in the squash, broth, hominy and seasonings. Bring to a boil. Reduce heat; cover and simmer for 15 minutes. Remove from the heat; stir in cream.

Yield: 4 servings.

Nutritional Analysis: 1-1/4 cups equals 203 calories, 9 g fat (5 g saturated fat), 28 mg cholesterol, 1,558 mg sodium, 29 g carbohydrate, 7 g fiber, 4 g protein.

Substitution Secret

Leftover white or wild rice can be added to this soup in place of the canned hominy.

Winter Squash Facts

Winter squash is an excellent source of vitamins A and C. It's also packed with potassium and fiber.

Use frozen cooked winter squash as a substitute for canned pumpkin in soups and baked goods. Or season with butter, salt and pepper for a savory side dish.

Bruschetta Polenta

PREP/TOTAL TIME: 10 min.

> 1 **package (1 pound) polenta, cut into 1/2-inch slices**
> 1 **tablespoon olive oil**
> 1 **cup bruschetta topping**
> 3 **tablespoons shredded Parmesan cheese**

In a large skillet, cook polenta slices in oil over medium heat for 2 minutes on each side or until golden. Place the bruschetta topping in a microwave-safe bowl; cover and cook on high for 1 minute. Spoon 1 tablespoon onto each slice of polenta; sprinkle with Parmesan cheese.

Yield: 6 servings.

Nutritional Analysis: 2 slices equals 116 calories, 5 g fat (1 g saturated fat), 2 mg cholesterol, 603 mg sodium, 16 g carbohydrate, 1 g fiber, 2 g protein.

Simple Bruschetta

You can find convenient bruschetta topping in the condiment aisle.

In addition to polenta, you can also use it to top slices of fresh French bread for an extra-easy appetizer. Or toss some with hot cooked pasta for a mouth-watering meatless meal.

If you want to take advantage of your bumper crop of tomatoes, why not make a bruschetta topping from scratch?

Seed and chop 2 large tomatoes; place in a bowl. Add 3 tablespoons minced fresh basil, 2 minced garlic cloves, 1 tablespoon olive oil, 1/2 teaspoon salt and 1/4 teaspoon pepper; mix well.

Blue Cheese Mashed Potatoes

PREP/TOTAL TIME: 5 min.

    1   package (2 pounds) refrigerated mashed potatoes
1/3 cup crumbled blue cheese

Heat potatoes according to package directions; stir in blue cheese. Serve immediately.

Yield: 6 servings.

Nutritional Analysis: 1/2 cup equals 178 calories, 2 g fat (1 g saturated fat), 6 mg cholesterol, 105 mg sodium, trace carbohydrate, 0 fiber, 2 g protein.

Easy Entree Ideas

When you crave comfort food, make mashed potatoes and meat loaf! (Turkey Meat Loaf is pictured below.)

Or you can pick up packaged marinated pork tenderloins from your grocer's meat case.

Bake the pork tenderloin at 425° for 20 minutes per pound. A 3/4- to 1-pound pork tenderloin can also be grilled for 15-20 minutes. The internal temperature of pork should be 160°.

Turkey Meat Loaf (p. 143)

Sesame Green Beans

PREP/TOTAL TIME: 15 min.

3/4 **pound fresh green beans, trimmed**
1/2 **cup water**
1 **tablespoon butter**
1 **tablespoon soy sauce**
2 **teaspoons sesame seeds, toasted**

In a large saucepan, bring beans and water to a boil. Reduce heat to medium; cover and cook for 5-7 minutes or until crisp-tender. Drain. Add the butter, soy sauce and sesame seeds; toss to coat.

Yield: 6 servings.

Nutritional Analysis: 1/2 cup equals 39 calories, 2 g fat (1 g saturated fat), 5 mg cholesterol, 181 mg sodium, 4 g carbohydrate, 2 g fiber, 1 g protein.

Don't Know Beans About Beans?

Green and wax beans can be used interchangeably in recipes. Look for brightly colored, straight, smooth pods that are free of blemishes. They should be crisp and have a firm, velvety feel. The seeds inside should be small.

Refrigerate unwashed beans in a sealed plastic bag for up to 3 days. Before using, snap off the stem end and the other end if desired. Run beans under cold running water to wash.

Colorful Pea Salad

PREP: 15 min. + chilling

2 medium carrots, chopped
1 package (16 ounces) frozen peas
1 celery rib, thinly sliced
1/4 cup cubed mozzarella cheese
1/4 cup chopped green onions
3 tablespoons buttermilk
1 tablespoon plain yogurt
1-1/2 teaspoons mayonnaise
1/2 teaspoon red wine vinegar
1/2 to 1 teaspoon dried basil
1/4 teaspoon sugar
1/8 teaspoon pepper

In a large saucepan, cook carrots in a small amount of boiling water for 2 minutes. Add peas; cook 5 minutes longer. Drain; rinse in cold water and drain again. Place in a bowl; add celery, cheese and onions.

In a small bowl, combine the remaining ingredients; pour over vegetable mixture and toss to coat. Cover and refrigerate for at least 1 hour before serving.

Yield: 6 servings.

Nutritional Analysis: 3/4 cup equals 97 calories, 2 g fat (1 g saturated fat), 5 mg cholesterol, 131 mg sodium, 14 g carbohydrate, 4 g fiber, 6 g protein.

Fresh Mozzarella Facts

Look for fresh mozzarella when making this colorful salad. Compared to the more firm texture of most commercially produced mozzarella, fresh mozzarella is soft and moist. The flavor is mild, delicate and somewhat milky.

Store fresh mozzarella in an airtight container in the refrigerator and use within 2 to 3 days.

Potluck Pleaser

When you need to bring a dish to pass to a picnic or potluck, make a double batch of Colorful Pea Salad! For added convenience, it can be prepared the night before.

Cauliflower Au Gratin

PREP/TOTAL TIME: 25 min.

- 1 **cup chicken broth**
- 1 **large head cauliflower, broken into florets**
- 1/4 **cup butter, cubed**
- 1/4 **cup seasoned bread crumbs**
- 1/2 **cup shredded Parmesan cheese**

In a large saucepan, bring broth to a boil. Add cauliflower. Reduce heat to medium; cover and cook for 15-18 minutes or until tender.

Meanwhile, in a small skillet, melt butter. Add bread crumbs; cook and stir for 3-5 minutes or until toasted and browned. Remove from the heat; stir in Parmesan cheese. Drain cauliflower; top with crumb mixture.

Yield: 6 servings.

Nutritional Analysis: 1 cup equals 150 calories, 10 g fat (6 g saturated fat), 25 mg cholesterol, 459 mg sodium, 11 g carbohydrate, 4 g fiber, 6 g protein.

Cauliflowerets Are Faster

For quicker preparation, head to the produce section and purchase two 12-ounce packages of ready-to-use cauliflower florets. Use 1-1/2 packages (or 18 ounces) for this recipe.

Tasty Topping

The buttered bread crumbs from Cauliflower Au Gratin can be used as a topping for a variety of vegetables.

Jicama-Radish Spinach Salad

PREP/TOTAL TIME: 15 min.

1/4 cup orange juice
2 tablespoons honey
2 tablespoons olive oil
1 tablespoon Dijon mustard
1 package (6 ounces) fresh baby spinach
1-1/2 cups julienned jicama
1/2 cup thinly sliced red onion
6 radishes, sliced

In a jar with a tight-fitting lid, combine the orange juice, honey, oil and mustard; shake well. In a large salad bowl, combine the spinach, jicama, onion and radishes. Drizzle with dressing and toss to coat.

Yield: 6 servings.

Nutritional Analysis: 1 cup equals 92 calories, 5 g fat (1 g saturated fat), 0 cholesterol, 88 mg sodium, 12 g carbohydrate, 3 g fiber, 1 g protein.

Just What Is Jicama?

Jicama is a legume that grows underground as a tuber. With a thin brown skin and white flesh, it resembles a turnip. Jicama is also known as a Mexican potato. Because it has a sweet flavor and a moist but crisp texture, jicama makes a nice addition to salads.

Look for firm, heavy jicamas with unblemished skin. Store whole jicamas in the refrigerator for up to 3 weeks. Wash, dry and peel before using.

Brussels Sprouts with Pecans

PREP/TOTAL TIME: 20 min.

1/2 cup chopped onion
2 teaspoons butter
1 pound fresh brussels sprouts, thinly sliced
1/3 cup chicken broth
1 tablespoon sugar
1/2 teaspoon salt
3 tablespoons chopped pecans, toasted

In a large skillet, saute onion in butter until tender. Add brussels sprouts; saute for 2 minutes. Add the broth, sugar and salt; cover and cook for 5 minutes or until sprouts are tender, stirring occasionally. Sprinkle with pecans.

Yield: 6 servings.

Nutritional Analysis: 1/2 cup equals 83 calories, 4 g fat (1 g saturated fat), 3 mg cholesterol, 280 mg sodium, 11 g carbohydrate, 3 g fiber, 3 g protein.

Grade A Chicken Entree

Honey Garlic Chicken is a standard entree you can turn to often.

Place 4 boneless skinless chicken breast halves in a greased 13-in. x 9-in. x 2-in. baking pan.

Combine 2 tablespoons honey, 2 tablespoons orange or lemon juice, 1 tablespoon vegetable oil, 1/2 teaspoon salt and a dash of pepper; pour over the chicken. Bake, uncovered, at 400° for 15 minutes.

Broil 4 to 6 in. from the heat for 5-7 minutes or until juices run clear, basting occasionally with the sauce.

Curried Barley with Raisins

PREP/TOTAL TIME: 20 min.

    1   cup chopped celery
    1   cup chopped onion
    1   teaspoon olive oil
    1   teaspoon minced garlic
  1/2   teaspoon curry powder
1-1/2   cups cooked barley
  1/4   cup slivered almonds, toasted
  1/4   cup raisins
  1/4   cup minced fresh parsley
  1/4   teaspoon salt
  1/4   teaspoon pepper

In a large skillet, saute celery and onion in oil for 8-10 minutes or until crisp-tender. Add the garlic and curry; saute for 1 minute. Warm barley in the microwave; stir into skillet. Add the remaining ingredients; cook and stir until heated through.

Yield: 4 servings.

Nutritional Analysis: 1/2 cup equals 172 calories, 5 g fat (1 g saturated fat), 0 cholesterol, 180 mg sodium, 30 g carbohydrate, 5 g fiber, 4 g protein.

Barley Basics

Generally, there are two types of barley available—hulled and pearl.

Hulled barley is the most nutritious because only the tough outer hull is removed. It's chewy and slow to cook.

With pearl barley, even more of the outer bran layer has been removed, leaving just the "pearl" inside. This is the most common form of barley found in grocery stores. It cooks in about an hour, which is faster than hulled barley, and is less chewy. Quick-cooking pearl barley cooks in 10 to 12 minutes.

Smashed Red Potatoes

PREP/TOTAL TIME: 25 min.

2 pounds red potatoes, cut into small wedges
1/4 cup minced fresh parsley
2 tablespoons olive oil
1 teaspoon salt
1/2 teaspoon pepper

Place the potatoes in a large saucepan and cover with water. Bring to a boil. Reduce heat to medium; cook, uncovered, for 15-20 minutes or until tender. Drain and place in a bowl. Coarsely mash the potatoes, adding the parsley, oil, salt and pepper.

Yield: 6 servings.

Nutritional Analysis: 3/4 cup equals 150 calories, 5 g fat (1 g saturated fat), 0 cholesterol, 404 mg sodium, 24 g carbohydrate, 3 g fiber, 3 g protein.

Red Potato Primer

Good quality red potatoes will be firm, smooth-skinned and have bright red coloring. It's normal for them to have a few shallow "eyes." Stay away from red potatoes that are soft, wrinkled, green-tinted or that have cuts.

Store red potatoes in a cool, dark, well-ventilated place for up to 2 weeks; do not refrigerate.

Sweet Potatoes 'n' Pears

PREP/TOTAL TIME: 30 min.

 9 cups cubed peeled sweet potatoes (about 4 medium)
 4 cups water
 1 can (15-1/4 ounces) pear halves, drained
 1/3 cup packed brown sugar
 1/4 cup butter, softened
 1/4 teaspoon ground cinnamon

Place the sweet potatoes in a shallow 3-qt. microwave-safe dish; add water. Cover and microwave on high for 18-20 minutes or until tender. Drain and place in a large mixing bowl. Add the remaining ingredients; beat until combined.

Yield: 8 servings.

Editor's Note: This recipe was tested in a 1,100-watt microwave.

Nutritional Analysis: 3/4 cup equals 286 calories, 6 g fat (4 g saturated fat), 15 mg cholesterol, 84 mg sodium, 57 g carbohydrate, 5 g fiber, 3 g protein.

Sweet Potato Secrets

Sweet potatoes (sometimes called yams) are available year-round, but November is the peak month. Look for firm, well-shaped sweet potatoes that are free of blemishes and dark knots. Skins that are darker tend to be sweeter and moister.

If stored in a cool, dark, well-ventilated place, they'll remain fresh for 2 weeks. If the temperature rises above 60°, they'll sprout sooner and become woody.

Scrub sweet potatoes with a vegetable brush before using. Remove eyes and sprouts. When working with large quantities, peel and place in cold water to prevent browning.

Once cooked, sweet potatoes can be stored in the refrigerator for up to 1 week.

Corn with a Kick

PREP/TOTAL TIME: 20 min.

1/4 cup chopped onion
1/4 cup chopped green pepper
  1 tablespoon butter
  2 cups whole kernel corn
1/4 cup diced tomato
  1 teaspoon salt
1/8 teaspoon pepper
Cayenne pepper to taste

In a large saucepan, saute onion and green pepper in butter until tender. Stir in the corn, tomato, salt, pepper and cayenne. Cover and simmer for 5-10 minutes or until heated through, stirring occasionally.

Yield: 4 servings.

Nutritional Analysis: 1/2 cup equals 125 calories, 4 g fat (2 g saturated fat), 8 mg cholesterol, 961 mg sodium, 16 g carbohydrate, 3 g fiber, 2 g protein.

Cutting Kernels From Corncobs

This slightly spicy side dish starts with uncooked kernels of corn. Stand one end of the cob on a cutting board. Starting at the top, run a sharp knife down the cob, cutting deeply to remove whole kernels.

One medium cob will give you about 1/2 cup kernels.

Mushroom Rice

PREP/TOTAL TIME: 25 min.

1   can (10-1/2 ounces) condensed beef broth, undiluted
3/4   cup uncooked long grain rice
1   jar (4-1/2 ounces) sliced mushrooms, drained
1/4   cup butter, melted
1/2   teaspoon garlic powder
1/2   teaspoon onion salt

In a 2-qt. microwave-safe dish, combine all ingredients. Cover and microwave on high for 4 minutes. Microwave at 50% power for 12 minutes. Let stand for 5-10 minutes. Stir before serving.

Yield: 4 servings.

Editor's Note: This recipe was tested in a 1,100-watt microwave.

Nutritional Analysis: 1/2 cup equals 250 calories, 12 g fat (7 g saturated fat), 31 mg cholesterol, 1,052 mg sodium, 30 g carbohydrate, 1 g fiber, 5 g protein.

Easy Stir-In Ideas

You can turn Mushroom Rice into a main dish by adding some roast beef from the deli.

Or prepare the recipe using chicken broth instead of beef broth; stir in cooked chicken, turkey or shrimp.

A green salad on the side easily rounds out the meal.

Strawberry Spinach Salad

PREP/TOTAL TIME: 10 min.

  1 package (10 ounces) fresh spinach, torn
  2 cups sliced fresh strawberries
  1 cup sliced fresh mushrooms
  1/3 cup real bacon bits
  1/3 cup raspberry vinaigrette

In a large salad bowl, combine the spinach, strawberries, mushrooms and bacon. Drizzle with vinaigrette and toss to coat.

Yield: 6 servings.

Nutritional Analysis: 1-1/4 cups equals 113 calories, 8 g fat (1 g saturated fat), 4 mg cholesterol, 348 mg sodium, 7 g carbohydrate, 3 g fiber, 4 g protein.

Homemade Raspberry Vinaigrette

Instead of purchasing raspberry vinaigrette, why not make your own?

Thaw and drain one package (10 ounces) frozen sweetened raspberries. Place in a blender or food processor; process until pureed. Strain to remove seeds. Return puree to blender.

Add 1/3 cup seedless raspberry jam, 2 tablespoons cider vinegar and 2 tablespoons lemon juice; cover and process until smooth. Add 1/2 cup olive oil, 1/8 teaspoon salt and a dash of pepper and nutmeg; Cover and process until blended. Makes 1-1/4 cups.

Use this vinaigrette in Strawberry Spinach Salad or a salad of fresh fruit. Raspberry vinaigrette also makes a nice marinade for boneless skinless chicken breasts.

Cherry Tomato Corn Salad

PREP/TOTAL TIME: 15 min.

1/4   cup minced fresh basil
  3   tablespoons olive oil
  2   teaspoons lime juice
  1   teaspoon sugar
1/2   teaspoon salt
1/4   teaspoon pepper
  2   cups frozen corn, thawed
  2   cups cherry tomatoes, halved
  1   cup chopped seeded peeled cucumber

In a jar with a tight-fitting lid, combine the basil, oil, lime juice, sugar, salt and pepper; shake well. In a large bowl, combine the corn, tomatoes and cucumber. Drizzle with dressing and toss to coat. Refrigerate until serving.

Yield: 6 servings.

Nutritional Analysis: 2/3 cup equals 125 calories, 7 g fat (1 g saturated fat), 0 cholesterol, 302 mg sodium, 15 g carbohydrate, 2 g fiber, 2 g protein.

A Lime Lesson

Although bottled lime juice is convenient, nothing beats the flavor of freshly squeezed juice.

Uncut limes stay fresh in the refrigerator for about 3 weeks. Once cut, cover with plastic wrap, refrigerate and use within 5 days. (One medium lime will give about 1-1/2 tablespoons juice.)

Purchase brightly colored limes with smooth skin. Avoid those that are hard and shriveled. Small brown areas won't affect the flavor.

Fresh Is Best

Cherry Tomato Corn Salad calls for frozen corn, so you can treat your family to a refreshing vegetable salad any time of year.

But in summer, consider taking advantage of fresh sweet corn off the cob. Quickly saute the kernels in a skillet for 5 minutes. Let cool slightly, then add to the salad.

Crisp Side Salad

PREP/TOTAL TIME: 10 min.

1/4	cup olive oil
2	tablespoons cider vinegar
4	teaspoons sugar
1/2	teaspoon salt
1/4	teaspoon pepper
4	cups torn salad greens
3/4	cup sliced zucchini
2	medium carrots, sliced
2	celery ribs, sliced
2	green onions, sliced
1/4	cup seasoned croutons
1	tablespoon whole almonds, toasted
1	tablespoon sesame seeds, toasted

In a jar with a tight-fitting lid, combine the oil, vinegar, sugar, salt and pepper; shake well. In a large salad bowl, combine the greens, zucchini, carrots, celery and onions. Drizzle with dressing and toss to coat. Top with croutons, almonds and sesame seeds.

Yield: 4 servings.

Nutritional Analysis: 1 cup equals 204 calories, 16 g fat (2 g saturated fat), trace cholesterol, 382 mg sodium, 14 g carbohydrate, 4 g fiber, 3 g protein.

Special Cheese Sandwiches

Serve Crisp Side Salad with cheesy grilled sandwiches that taste just like lasagna!

Combine 1/4 cup sour cream, 2 tablespoons chopped onion, 1/2 teaspoon dried oregano and 1/4 teaspoon seasoned salt; spread on four slices of bread. Top each with four bacon halves, two tomato slices and a slice of mozzarella cheese; top with remaining bread.

In a skillet over medium heat, melt 2 tablespoons butter. Cook sandwiches on both sides until bread is lightly browned and the cheese is melted, adding more butter if necessary.

Bulgur with Pine Nuts

PREP/TOTAL TIME: 20 min.

    1 cup uncooked bulgur
    2 cups chicken broth
    3 tablespoons chopped green onions
  1/4 cup pine nuts, toasted

In a large saucepan, combine the bulgur, broth and onions; bring to a boil over high heat. Reduce heat; cover and simmer for 15-18 minutes or until broth is absorbed. Add pine nuts; stir to combine.

Yield: 4 servings.

Nutritional Analysis: 1/2 cup equals 177 calories, 5 g fat (1 g saturated fat), 0 cholesterol, 472 mg sodium, 29 g carbohydrate, 7 g fiber, 7 g protein.

Bulgur Wheat Basics

Bulgur wheat is a light nutty grain that can be found in the natural foods section of your local grocery store.

No Time for Toasting?

Although toasting the pine nuts adds great flavor to this side dish, you can skip that step and use untoasted pine nuts if time is short and you need to get dinner made quickly.

Cider-Glazed Carrots

PREP/TOTAL TIME: 30 min.

3 cups julienned fresh carrots
2 tablespoons butter
1 tablespoon brown sugar
1/2 cup apple cider *or* juice
3 tablespoons water
1 teaspoon Dijon mustard

In a large skillet, saute carrots in butter for 5 minutes. Add brown sugar. Cook and stir for 1 minute or until the sugar is dissolved.

Stir in the cider, water and mustard. Bring to a boil. Reduce heat; cover and simmer for 10-12 minutes or until carrots are crisp-tender. Uncover and cook 3 minutes longer. Stir to coat carrots with the glaze.

Yield: 4 servings.

Nutritional Analysis: 1/2 cup equals 119 calories, 6 g fat (4 g saturated fat), 15 mg cholesterol, 126 mg sodium, 17 g carbohydrate, 3 g fiber, 1 g protein.

Time-Saving Tip

To make your preparation time quicker, use packaged shredded carrots. Then simply place all of the ingredients in a skillet and bring to a boil. Cover and simmer for 10-12 minutes. Uncover and cook for 3 minutes more or until sauce is thickened.

Even families on the go can indulge in dessert with this chapter's speedy sweets!

Mousse in Waffle Bowls (p. 298)

In-a-Dash **Desserts**

In-a-Dash
Desserts

In-a-Dash **Desserts**

Lemon Blueberry Pizza

PREP: 10 min. **BAKE:** 15 min. + cooling

1 package (18 ounces) refrigerated sugar cookie
dough
1 package (8 ounces) cream cheese, softened
2 tablespoons sugar
1 carton (6 ounces) lemon yogurt
2 cups fresh blueberries

Press cookie dough onto an ungreased 12-in. pizza pan. Bake at 350° for 12-15 minutes or until golden brown. Cool on a wire rack.

In a small mixing bowl, beat cream cheese and sugar until smooth; stir in yogurt. Spread over crust to within 1/2 in. of edges. Sprinkle with blueberries. Cut into wedges. Refrigerate leftovers.

Yield: 8 servings.

Nutritional Analysis: 1 piece equals 431 calories, 23 g fat (10 g saturated fat), 51 mg cholesterol, 367 mg sodium, 51 g carbohydrate, 1 g fiber, 6 g protein.

Blueberry Basics

Purchase fresh blueberries that are plump, firm and uniform in size. They should have shiny, silver-frosted skin. One pint equals about 2 cups.

Refrigerate blueberries in a covered container for up to 10 days. Before using, wash the berries and remove any stems.

Blueberries are great to freeze and have on hand for a variety of recipes. Wash the berries; blot dry with paper towels. Place in a single layer in a 15-in. x 11-in. jelly roll pan; freeze. When hard, transfer to a heavy-duty resealable plastic bag and freeze for up to 9 months. There's no need to thaw the berries before adding to the batter for baked goods.

Tasty Tiramisu

PREP/TOTAL TIME: 15 min.

6 individual round sponge cakes
6 teaspoons strong brewed coffee
1 package (8 ounces) cream cheese, softened
1/2 cup sugar
1/3 cup chocolate syrup
1 cup whipped topping, *divided*
3 teaspoons baking cocoa
1/4 teaspoon ground cinnamon

Place sponge cakes on dessert plates; drizzle with coffee. In a small mixing bowl, beat the cream cheese and sugar until smooth. Beat in the chocolate syrup. Fold in 3/4 cup whipped topping just until combined. Spoon over cakes. Dollop with remaining whipped topping; sprinkle with cocoa and cinnamon.

Yield: 6 servings.

Nutritional Analysis: 1 serving equals 367 calories, 16 g fat (11 g saturated fat), 73 mg cholesterol, 196 mg sodium, 50 g carbohydrate, 1 g fiber, 5 g protein.

Save Some Coffee

After brewing a pot of coffee in the morning, set aside 6 teaspoons for making this recipe in the evening. Cover and refrigerate until ready to use.

What Is Tiramisu?

Tiramisu is Italian for "pick me up" and that's just what this dessert does! The classic dessert features ladyfingers and sweetened mascarpone cheese. This simply delicious version relies on individual sponge cakes and sweetened cream cheese.

Cran-Orange Sponge Dessert

PREP/TOTAL TIME: 20 min.

>   1   tablespoon cornstarch
> 1-1/2 cups cranberry juice
>   2   tablespoons light corn syrup
>   2   medium navel oranges, peeled and chopped
>   1/3   cup dried cranberries
>   1   cinnamon stick (3 inches)
>   6   individual cream-filled sponge cakes, cut
>   into 1/2-inch cubes
> Whipped cream, optional

In a large saucepan, combine cornstarch and cranberry juice until smooth; bring to a boil over medium-high heat, stirring constantly. Stir in corn syrup until blended. Cook and stir for 2 minutes or until thickened.

Stir in the oranges, cranberries and cinnamon stick; simmer, uncovered, for 10 minutes or until the berries pop. Discard cinnamon stick. Divide cake cubes among four dessert dishes; top each with 1/2 cup fruit sauce. Garnish with whipped cream if desired. Serve warm.

Yield: 4 servings.

Nutritional Analysis: One serving equals 385 calories, 7 g fat (2 g saturated fat), 10 mg cholesterol, 248 mg sodium, 81 g carbohydrate, 3 g fiber, 3 g protein.

Sweetened Whipped Cream

Consider serving individual servings of Cran-Orange Sponge Dessert with a dollop of sweetened whipped cream.

To sweeten whipping cream, add 2 tablespoons confectioners' sugar to each cup of heavy whipping cream before whipping. In a mixing bowl, whip on high speed until stiff peaks form.

Chocolate Peanut Grahams

PREP: 10 min. + chilling

  4   cinnamon graham crackers, broken into quarters
1/4   cup creamy peanut butter
  1   cup (6 ounces) semisweet chocolate chips
  3   teaspoons shortening

Spread half of the graham cracker quarters with peanut butter; top with remaining crackers. In a microwave-safe bowl, melt chocolate chips and shortening; stir until smooth. Dip the crackers into chocolate; place on a waxed paper-lined pan. Refrigerate until set.

Yield: 8 cookies.

Nutritional Analysis: 2 cookies equals 376 calories, 24 g fat (10 g saturated fat), 0 cholesterol, 164 mg sodium, 41 g carbohydrate, 4 g fiber, 7 g protein.

Easy Assembly

Children will get a kick out of making these chocolate peanut treats. Get the ingredients together and have the kids assemble them while you're preparing dinner.

Consider making a double or triple batch, then freeze some for a fast snack from the freezer.

Substitution Secret

Regular graham crackers can be used in place of the cinnamon graham crackers.

Peaches 'n' Cream Crisp

PREP/TOTAL TIME: 10 min.

3 cups fresh *or* frozen sliced peaches
4 teaspoons butterscotch ice cream topping
4 tablespoons granola cereal without raisins
4 scoops vanilla ice cream

Place the peaches in four 8-oz. ramekins or custard cups. Top with butterscotch topping and granola. Microwave, uncovered, on high for 2-3 minutes or until bubbly. Top with ice cream.

Yield: 4 servings.

Editor's Note: This recipe was tested in a 1,100-watt microwave.

Nutritional Analysis: 1 serving equals 241 calories, 9 g fat (5 g saturated fat), 29 mg cholesterol, 94 mg sodium, 39 g carbohydrate, 3 g fiber, 4 g protein.

Fresh Peach Facts

When buying peaches, select those that are fragrant and give slightly to pressure. Don't purchase peaches that are hard, bruised or green.

To ripen peaches, place in a brown paper lunch bag along with an apple. Poke several holes in the bag. Keep at room temperature until ripened.

Refrigerate ripe peaches in a plastic bag for up to 5 days.

One pound equals about 4 medium or 2-3/4 cups sliced.

Preparation Pointer

If you're using frozen peaches in this recipe, you'll likely need to microwave for a slightly longer time.

Mousse in Waffle Bowls

PREP: 15 min. + chilling

    5   squares (1 ounce *each*) white baking chocolate
    1   teaspoon shortening
    4   ice cream waffle bowls
    2   packages (2.8 ounces *each*) chocolate mousse mix
1-1/3   cups cold milk
Whipped topping and sliced fresh strawberries, optional

In a microwave-safe bowl, melt chocolate and shortening; stir until smooth. Brush over the inside of waffle bowls. Refrigerate for 5 minutes or until chocolate is set.

Meanwhile, prepare mousse according to package directions, using 1-1/3 cups milk. Spoon into waffle bowls. Refrigerate for 1 hour or until serving. Garnish with whipped topping and strawberries if desired.

Yield: 4 servings.

Nutritional Analysis: One serving equals 513 calories, 27 g fat (16 g saturated fat), 19 mg cholesterol, 252 mg sodium, 59 g carbohydrate, trace fiber, 10 g protein.

Strawberry Basics

Although it seems supermarkets carry strawberries year-round, the prime season actually begins in mid-May, peaks in June and is finished by mid-July.

Purchase brightly colored berries that are plump and fragrant and that have a fresh green hull attached. Avoid strawberries with green or white color or those that appear mushy or shriveled.

Store strawberries in a shallow container on a paper towel in the refrigerator for up to 3 days. Wash just before using. For optimum flavor, serve at room temperature.

One pint of strawberries will yield 1-1/2 to 2 cups sliced.

Taste of Home's Weeknight Cooking Made Easy

Apple Gingerbread Cake

PREP: 5 min.   **BAKE:** 25 min. + cooling

1   package (14-1/2 ounces) gingerbread cake/
    cookie mix
1-1/4   cups water
1   egg
1   cup chopped peeled apple
1/2   cup chopped pecans
2   tablespoons brown sugar

In a large mixing bowl, beat the cake mix, water and egg until combined. Add apple; stir to combine. Pour into a greased 11-in. x 7-in. x 2-in. baking dish. Combine the pecans and brown sugar; sprinkle over the top.

Bake at 350° for 23-25 minutes or until a toothpick inserted near the center comes out clean. Cool on a wire rack.

Yield: 9 servings.

Nutritional Analysis: 1 piece equals 272 calories, 12 g fat (2 g saturated fat), 24 mg cholesterol, 308 mg sodium, 40 g carbohydrate, 2 g fiber, 3 g protein.

All About Apples

For all-purpose apples that are good for both cooking and eating raw, pick up any of these varieties: Cortland, Empire, Golden Delicious, Granny Smith, Jonagold, Jonathon, McIntosh and Rome Beauty.

Apples discolor quickly, so don't peel and chop until just before adding to the batter for Apple Gingerbread Cake. When using chopped apples in a fruit salad, toss with a little lemon juice to prevent browning. One large apple will yield about 1 cup chopped.

White Chip Cookies

PREP/TOTAL TIME: 25 min.

1 package (9 ounces) devil's food cake mix
2 tablespoons baking cocoa
1 egg
2 tablespoons cream cheese, softened
1 tablespoon milk
3/4 cup vanilla *or* white chips

In a small mixing bowl, combine the cake mix, cocoa, egg, cream cheese and milk; mix well (batter will be thick). Stir in chips. Drop by tablespoonfuls 2 in. apart onto a greased baking sheet. Bake at 350° for 14-16 minutes or until a toothpick comes out clean.

Yield: 1 dozen.

Nutritional Analysis: 2 cookies equals 328 calories, 14 g fat (7 g saturated fat), 46 mg cholesterol, 372 mg sodium, 47 g carbohydrate, 1 g fiber, 5 g protein.

The Choice for Chocolate Lovers!

If your family is a fan of chocolate, use semi-sweet chocolate chips in place of the vanilla or white chips.

Preparation Pointer

This recipe makes the perfect-sized batch. To make 2 dozen, simply double the ingredients.

In-a-Dash **Desserts**

Pineapple Orange Cheesecake

PREP/TOTAL TIME: 20 min.

- 2 cups cubed fresh pineapple
- 2 tablespoons brown sugar
- 2 tablespoons butter
- 1/3 cup orange marmalade
- 1 package (30 ounces) frozen New York-style cheesecake, thawed

Whipped topping, optional

In a large skillet, saute pineapple and brown sugar in butter for 8 minutes. Spread orange marmalade over cheesecake; top with pineapple mixture. Garnish with whipped topping if desired.

Yield: 6 servings.

Nutritional Analysis: 1 slice equals 575 calories, 36 g fat (16 g saturated fat), 88 mg cholesterol, 344 mg sodium, 59 g carbohydrate, 1 g fiber, 8 g protein.

Easy Cheesecake Toppings

Frozen cheesecake is a great dessert to have in the freezer both for weeknight treats as well as for weekend company. Enjoy slices plain or garnish with an assortment of toppings.

Open a can of cherry, apple or blueberry pie filling and spoon some over slices. Drizzle with chocolate syrup or hot fudge sauce. Or simply sprinkle fresh fruit on top.

You can also make a quick raspberry sauce. Thaw a 10-ounce package of frozen sweetened raspberries in the microwave. Transfer to a blender; puree until smooth. Press through a sieve; discard seeds. Cover and refrigerate sauce until ready to use.

Cheery Cherry Parfaits

PREP: 10 min. + chilling

2 cups cold milk
1 package (3.3 ounces) instant white chocolate pudding mix
8 date oatmeal cookies, coarsely crumbled
1 cup cherry pie filling

In a bowl, whisk milk and pudding mix for 2 minutes. Let stand for 2 minutes or until soft-set. Spoon 1/4 cup pudding into each of four parfait glasses.

Layer each with 1/3 cup cookie crumbs and 1/4 cup pie filling. Top with the remaining pudding and cookie crumbs. Refrigerate for 1 hour before serving.

Yield: 4 servings.

Nutritional Analysis: 1 parfait equals 335 calories, 6 g fat (2 g saturated fat), 7 mg cholesterol, 551 mg sodium, 68 g carbohydrate, 2 g fiber, 3 g protein.

Serving Suggestion

Instead of making individual Cheery Cherry Parfaits, you can layer the pudding, cookies and pie filling in a clear glass bowl for an impressive yet timeless trifle. It's so delicious, even guests will be impressed by this in-a-hurry dessert!

Substitution Secret

For a change of pace, layer the white chocolate pudding mix with apple, peach or blueberry pie filling.

If you use strawberry pie filling, replace the white chocolate pudding with chocolate fudge pudding.

Cranberry Upside-Down Cakes

PREP/TOTAL TIME: 30 min.

1 package (9 ounces) devil's food cake mix
1 egg
1/2 cup cold water, *divided*
3 tablespoons butter, cut into 6 pieces
1/3 cup packed brown sugar
1/3 cup chopped walnuts
1/3 cup flaked coconut
6 tablespoons whole-berry cranberry sauce
Whipped cream, optional

In a small mixing bowl, combine the cake mix, egg and 1/4 cup cold water. Beat for 2 minutes on medium speed. Add the remaining water; beat 2 minutes longer. Set aside.

Generously grease six 6-oz. custard cups; place a piece of butter in each cup. Combine the brown sugar, walnuts and coconut; sprinkle into cups. Spread each with cranberry sauce; top with cake batter. Bake at 375° for 20-25 minutes or until cake springs back when lightly touched. Cool on a wire rack for 5 minutes before inverting onto dessert plates. Garnish with whipped cream if desired.

Yield: 6 servings.

Nutritional Analysis: 1 serving equals 375 calories, 16 g fat (7 g saturated fat), 51 mg cholesterol, 357 mg sodium, 55 g carbohydrate, 2 g fiber, 5 g protein.

Preparation Pointer

If time gets away from you while preparing this dessert and you forget to remove the cakes from the custard cups after cooling for 5 minutes, warm the cakes in the microwave for a short time. Then invert onto dessert plates and garnish as desired.

Fruit Drop Candies

PREP: 10 min. + chilling

    2   packages (6 ounces *each*) white baking chocolate, chopped
    1   package (8 ounces) mixed dried fruit
 1/2   cup chopped slivered almonds

In a microwave-safe bowl, melt the white chocolate; stir until smooth. Stir in the fruit and almonds until well coated. Drop by tablespoonfuls into 16 mounds onto a waxed paper-lined pan. Refrigerate until set.

Yield: 16 pieces.

Nutritional Analysis: 2 pieces equals 348 calories, 19 g fat (9 g saturated fat), 9 mg cholesterol, 50 mg sodium, 43 g carbohydrate, 3 g fiber, 5 g protein.

Faster Preparation

This recipe for Fruit Drop Candies is already a snap. But for even faster preparation, allow the candies to set up in the freezer instead of the refrigerator. They'll be ready in about 5 minutes.

Kids in the Kitchen

While you're preparing dinner, have the kids mix these candy ingredients together and drop mounds onto waxed paper.

Boston Cream Angel Cake

PREP: 10 min. + chilling

2   cups plus 1 tablespoon cold milk, *divided*
1   package (3.4 ounces) instant French vanilla pudding mix
1   prepared angel food cake (16 ounces)
1   cup hot fudge ice cream topping

In a bowl, whisk 2 cups milk and pudding mix for 2 minutes. Let stand for 2 minutes or until soft-set. Split cake into three horizontal layers; place bottom layer on a serving plate. Spread with half of the pudding. Repeat layers. Replace cake top. Cover and refrigerate until serving.

In a small microwave-safe bowl, heat hot fudge topping; stir in remaining milk. Drizzle over cake, allowing it to drip down the sides. Refrigerate leftovers.

Yield: 8 servings.

Nutritional Analysis: 1 piece equals 357 calories, 5 g fat (2 g saturated fat), 8 mg cholesterol, 673 mg sodium, 71 g carbohydrate, 2 g fiber, 7 g protein.

Other Flavor Combinations

Boston Cream Angel Cake is an easy and clever way to dress up purchased angel food cake for a delectable dessert in no time.

To change this cake to your family's liking, try different flavors of instant pudding or different ice cream toppings.

The hot fudge ice cream topping would also pair well with chocolate, banana cream or pistachio pudding mix.

Instead of French vanilla pudding, use cheesecake or lemon pudding. Then top slices with strawberry ice cream topping.

You could also try butterscotch pudding with caramel topping or coconut cream pudding with pineapple ice cream sauce.

Rice Pudding Tartlets

PREP/TOTAL TIME: 25 min.

10 large marshmallows
1 tablespoon butter
1-1/2 cups crisp rice cereal
1/4 cup flaked coconut
1 carton (16 ounces) prepared rice pudding
1 tablespoon cold milk
1/2 cup golden raisins
Ground cinnamon, optional

In a large microwave-safe bowl, heat the marshmallows and butter until melted; stir until smooth. Stir in the cereal and coconut until combined. Coat six 6-oz. custard cups with nonstick cooking spray; press 1/4 cup cereal mixture onto the bottom and up the sides of each cup. Let stand for 15 minutes.

In a bowl, combine the pudding, milk and raisins. Remove cereal cups from custard cups; fill with pudding mixture. Sprinkle with cinnamon if desired.

Yield: 6 servings.

Editor's Note: This recipe was tested in a 1,100-watt microwave.

Nutritional Analysis: 1 serving equals 227 calories, 6 g fat (4 g saturated fat), 16 mg cholesterol, 153 mg sodium, 42 g carbohydrate, 2 g fiber, 4 g protein.

Preparation Pointers

Prepared rice pudding can be found in the refrigerated deli section of your local grocery store.

These crisp rice cereal nests can also be used for vanilla or chocolate pudding, an assortment of ice cream flavors and even fresh fruit salad with real kid appeal!

Hazelnut Cheesecake Dessert

PREP: 20 min. + chilling

  1 package (1-1/2 ounces) ice cream cake cones
3/4 cup chocolate hazelnut spread
  1 package (8 ounces) cream cheese, softened
1/2 cup sugar
  1 carton (8 ounces) frozen whipped topping, thawed
  1 package (2-1/2 ounces) chopped hazelnuts, toasted

Place ice cream cones in a large resealable bag; crush with a rolling pin. Transfer to a bowl. In a small microwave-safe bowl, heat the hazelnut spread on high for 30 seconds or until it achieves spreading consistency. Add 1/2 cup spread to the crushed cones. Using a metal spatula, press mixture into a greased 9-in. square pan.

In a small mixing bowl, beat the cream cheese and sugar until light and fluffy. Fold in whipped topping just until combined. Spread two-thirds of cream cheese mixture over the crust. Stir the remaining hazelnut spread into the remaining cream cheese mixture. Spread over cream cheese layer; sprinkle with nuts. Refrigerate overnight.

Yield: 9 servings.

Nutritional Analysis: 1 piece equals 393 calories, 25 g fat (11 g saturated fat), 28 mg cholesterol, 91 mg sodium, 38 g carbohydrate, 2 g fiber, 5 g protein.

Do-Ahead Dessert

Because this dessert needs time to refrigerate overnight, it's a real boon to busy cooks. Simply assemble and chill the night before. Then the next day, dessert is ready to serve right after dinner!

Searching for the Spread?

Chocolate hazelnut spread can be found near the peanut butter in your grocery store.

Strawberry Granola Squares

PREP: 5 min.   **BAKE:** 25 min. + cooling

1-1/2	cups granola cereal without raisins
3/4	cup all-purpose flour
1/3	cup packed brown sugar
1/2	teaspoon ground cinnamon
5	tablespoons cold butter
1	cup strawberry preserves

In a large bowl, combine the granola, flour, brown sugar and cinnamon; cut in butter until crumbly. Set aside a third of the mixture for topping. Press remaining mixture into a well-greased 9-in. square baking pan. Bake at 375° for 10 minutes.

Spread preserves over crust; sprinkle with reserved granola mixture. Bake 15 minutes longer or until filling is bubbly around the edges. Cool on a wire rack. Cut into squares. Store in the refrigerator.

Yield: 16 squares.

Nutritional Analysis: 2 squares equals 349 calories, 11 g fat (5 g saturated fat), 19 mg cholesterol, 129 mg sodium, 60 g carbohydrate, 2 g fiber, 4 g protein.

Distinguishing Different Toppings

Jam, jelly and preserves are all made from fruit mixed with sugar and pectin. The difference between them comes in the form that the fruit takes.

In jam, the fruit comes in the form of fruit pulp or crushed fruit. For jelly, the fruit is in fruit juice. The fruit in preserves is in the form of chunks.

Warm Banana Crepes

PREP/TOTAL TIME: 10 min.

1/2 cup butter
1/2 cup packed brown sugar
4 medium ripe bananas, halved lengthwise
4 crepes (9 inches)

In a large skillet, melt butter. Add brown sugar; heat and stir until sugar is dissolved. Add bananas; cook until light golden brown, turning once. In an ungreased skillet, heat crepes for 10 seconds on each side or until warm.

Place two banana halves in the center of each crepe. Fold sides over filling and roll up; drizzle with brown sugar mixture.

Yield: 4 servings.

Nutritional Analysis: 1 filled crepe equals 457 calories, 24 g fat (15 g saturated fat), 67 mg cholesterol, 324 mg sodium, 62 g carbohydrate, 3 g fiber, 2 g protein.

Preparation Pointer

Ready-to-use crepes can be found near the berries in a store's produce section. Freeze any leftover crepes for another use.

Substitution Secret

If you can't find prepared crepes at the store, you can substitute flour tortillas instead. Heat according to package directions before filling with the banana halves.

In-a-Dash **Desserts**

Dessert Waffles

PREP/TOTAL TIME: 15 min.

   6 **frozen waffles**
   1 **cup (6 ounces) semisweet chocolate chips**
   2 **teaspoons shortening**
3/4 **cup strawberry pie filling**
   6 **scoops vanilla ice cream**

Toast waffles according to package directions. Meanwhile, in a microwave-safe bowl, combine chocolate chips and shortening. Microwave, uncovered, at 50% power for 1 minute or until chips are melted; stir until smooth. Drizzle over waffles; let stand for 5 minutes or until hardened. Top each with 2 tablespoons pie filling and a scoop of ice cream.

Yield: 6 servings.

Nutritional Analysis: 1 waffle with 1/2 cup ice cream equals 403 calories, 20 g fat (10 g saturated fat), 40 mg cholesterol, 329 mg sodium, 56 g carbohydrate, 3 g fiber, 6 g protein.

Flavorful Twists

For a tasty variation, top apple cinnamon waffles with caramel ice cream topping, apple pie filling and scoops of cinnamon ice cream.

Or use blueberry waffles, blueberry pie filling and whipped topping. No ice cream topping is needed.

Swap Out the Sauce

Instead of melting chocolate chips, top the waffles with chocolate hard shell ice cream topping. You can also simply substitute chocolate syrup or hot fudge ice cream topping.

Fruity Puff Pastries

PREP/TOTAL TIME: 30 min.

  1   package (10 ounces) frozen puff pastry shells
  6   medium pears, peeled and sliced
1/4 cup butter, cubed
1/3 cup packed brown sugar
1/2 teaspoon ground cinnamon
1/4 cup heavy whipping cream
1-1/2 cups fresh raspberries
Whipped cream and additional raspberries, optional

Bake pastry shells according to package directions. In a large skillet, saute the pears in butter, brown sugar and cinnamon for 5 minutes or until pears are tender. Add the cream. Cook and stir for 2 minutes or until thickened. Gently stir in the raspberries. Remove top of pastry shells; fill with fruit mixture. Garnish with whipped cream and additional raspberries if desired.

Yield: 6 servings.

Nutritional Analysis: 1 serving equals 475 calories, 26 g fat (10 g saturated fat), 34 mg cholesterol, 221 mg sodium, 60 g carbohydrate, 8 g fiber, 4 g protein.

Fresh Raspberry Facts

Look for brightly colored, plump raspberries without hulls attached.

When you get home, discard any raspberries that are soft, shriveled or moldy. To avoid bruising, place in a single layer on a paper towel-lined baking sheet. They'll stay fresh in the refrigerator for up to 3 days. Quickly rinse just before using.

One-half pint of raspberries yields about 1 cup.

Make-Ahead Pointer

Puff pastry shells can be baked and stored in an airtight container for up to 2 days. Before using, you can reheat them in a 400° oven for 5 minutes.

Lemon Strawberry Tarts

PREP: 5 min. **BAKE:** 15 min. + cooling

 1 package (18 ounces) refrigerated sugar cookie dough
3/4 cup chilled lemon curd
 6 large fresh strawberries, sliced
Whipped cream

Cut the cookie dough into 1/2-in. slices. Place 2 in. apart on ungreased baking sheets. Bake at 350° for 11-12 minutes or until lightly browned. Remove to wire racks to cool.

Spread six cookies with 2 tablespoons lemon curd. Garnish with strawberries and whipped cream. Save remaining cookies for another use.

Yield: 6 tarts.

Nutritional Analysis: 1 tart equals 267 calories, 8 g fat (2 g saturated fat), 38 mg cholesterol, 150 mg sodium, 46 g carbohydrate, trace fiber, 1 g protein.

Look for Lemon Curd

Lemon curd is located near the jams and jellies at your grocery store.

Preparation Pointers

You'll have leftover cookies after baking the refrigerated cookie dough. Either put them in the cookie jar for a quick snack, or freeze them and make this dessert again the following week. For an even easier dessert, purchase bakery sugar cookies instead of baking them yourself.

Tropical Pound Cake

PREP/TOTAL TIME: 15 min.

4   tablespoons butter, *divided*
1   package (10-3/4 ounces) frozen pound cake, thawed and cut into 12 slices
2   cans (15-1/4 ounces *each*) mixed tropical fruit, drained
2   tablespoons honey
6   tablespoons flaked coconut, toasted
Pomegranate seeds, optional

Melt 2 tablespoons butter; lightly brush over one side of each cake slice. Place buttered side up in a foil-lined 15-in. x 10-in. x 1-in. baking pan. Broil 3-4 in. from the heat for 1-2 minutes or until golden brown.

In a large skillet, melt remaining butter; add fruit. Cook and stir over medium heat for 5 minutes or until heated through. Stir in honey; cook for 2 minutes. Place two cake slices on each of six dessert plates. Top each with 1/2 cup fruit mixture; sprinkle with coconut. Garnish with pomegranate seeds if desired.

Yield: 6 servings.

Nutritional Analysis: 1 serving equals 433 calories, 18 g fat (11 g saturated fat), 93 mg cholesterol, 280 mg sodium, 67 g carbohydrate, 3 g fiber, 4 g protein.

Pretty Pomegranate Garnish

Pomegranate seeds add a nice garnish to Tropical Pound Cake. Here's how to extract the seeds from this exotic fruit.

Cut off the crown and score the fruit into quarters. Soak the fruit in a large bowl of cold water for 5 minutes. Holding the fruit under water, break the scored sections apart with your fingers. Then separate the seed clusters from the skin and membranes. Discard the skin and the membranes; dry the seeds on paper towels.

Peanut Butter Bars

PREP: 15 min. + chilling

1 cup sugar
1 cup light corn syrup
1-1/2 cups creamy peanut butter
6 cups Special K
2 cups (12 ounces) semisweet chocolate chips
1 cup butterscotch chips

In a Dutch oven, bring the sugar and corn syrup to a boil over medium heat; cook and stir for 2-3 minutes or until sugar is dissolved. Remove from the heat. Stir in peanut butter until combined. Add cereal; mix well.

Using a metal spatula, press mixture into an ungreased 13-in. x 9-in. x 2-in. pan. In a microwave-safe bowl, melt the chocolate and butterscotch chips; stir until smooth. Spread over cereal mixture. Refrigerate until set. Cut into bars.

Yield: 4 dozen.

Nutritional Analysis: 2 bars equals 316 calories, 15 g fat (7 g saturated fat), 1 mg cholesterol, 157 mg sodium, 43 g carbohydrate, 2 g fiber, 7 g protein.

Clues for Easy Cutting

Refrigerating these Peanut Butter Bars makes them easier to cut. (However, if the bars have been refrigerated for longer than 1 hour, let them stand at room temperature for 10 to 15 minutes before cutting.)

To make cutting even simpler, line the baking pan with foil before pressing the mixture into the pan. When the bars are set, lift the foil from the pan. Pull away the foil and cut into bars.

Freezer Facts

These bars freeze well, so you can keep squares on hand for tucking into lunches as a special treat. They're also a nice snack to have in the freezer for unexpected guests.

Apricot Pumpkin Cake

PREP: 5 min.   **BAKE:** 25 min. + cooling

1   cup chopped dried apricots
1   package (14 ounces) pumpkin quick bread/ muffin mix
1   cup water
2   eggs
3   tablespoons vegetable oil
1   can (15 ounces) apricot halves, drained
1   can (16 ounces) cream cheese frosting
1/2 cup chopped pecans

Set aside 1/2 cup dried apricots for garnish. In a small bowl, soak remaining apricots in hot water for 5 minutes; drain well. Puree in a food processor or blender.

In a large mixing bowl, combine the quick bread mix, water, eggs, oil and pureed apricots. Stir in canned apricots. Pour into a greased 11-in. x 7-in. x 2-in. baking dish.

Bake at 375° for 22-27 minutes or until a toothpick inserted near the center comes out clean. Cool on a wire rack. Frost cake with cream cheese frosting; sprinkle with pecans and reserved apricots. Refrigerate leftovers.

Yield: 9 servings.

Nutritional Analysis: 1 piece equals 568 calories, 21 g fat (3 g saturated fat), 47 mg cholesterol, 381 mg sodium, 90 g carbohydrate, 3 g fiber, 5 g protein.

Easy Cream Cheese Frosting

When time allows, make your own cream cheese frosting and refrigerate it until ready to use. Get things started by softening the cream cheese in the microwave.

In a mixing bowl, beat 3/4 cup softened butter, 2 packages (3 ounces *each*) softened cream cheese and 1 teaspoon vanilla until smooth. Gradually beat in 3 cups confectioners' sugar.

Revive Dried Fruit

Before dried fruit is used in cooking, a recipe may require you to reconstitute it…or soak it in a hot liquid. Doing this restores the moisture that was taken out when the fruit was dried, resulting in plump, juicy fruit.

Refrigerator & Freezer Facts

Refrigerators and freezers are terrific tools for creating timeless meals. Follow these guidelines for properly storing food and for keeping your freezer organized.

Refrigerating and Freezing Meat, Poultry and Fish

Food	Refrigerator (34° to 40°)	Freezer (0° or below)
Meat (beef, pork, lamb)		
Chops	3 to 5 days	4 to 6 months
Ground meat or stew meat	1 to 2 days	3 to 4 months
Roasts	3 to 5 days	4 to 12 months
Sausage, fresh	1 to 2 days	1 to 2 months
Steaks	3 to 5 days	6 to 12 months
Leftover, cooked meats/casseroles	1 to 4 days	2 to 3 months
Process meats		
Bacon	7 days*	1 month
Ham	3 to 5 days	1 to 2 months
Hot Dogs	7 days*	1 to 2 months
Luncheon meat	3 to 5 days*	1 to 2 months
Poultry (chicken, turkey)		
Whole	1 to 2 days	1 year
Pieces	1 to 2 days	9 months
Leftover, cooked poultry/casseroles	1 to 4 days	1 to 4 months
Fish & Seafood		
Lean fish (cod, sole, halibut, orange roughy, flounder)	1 to 2 days	1 year
Fatty fish (catfish, perch, salmon, whitefish)	1 to 2 days	2 to 3 months
Scallops/shrimp, cooked	3 to 4 days	3 months
Scallops/shrimp, uncooked	1 to 2 days	3 to 6 months
Leftover, cooked fish/seafood	3 to 4 days	3 to 6 months

*Dates apply to opened vacuum-sealed packages. Unopened vacuum-sealed packages can be stored in the refrigerator for 2 weeks or until the "use by" or "sell by" date expires.

Properly Freezing Foods

- Keep a thermometer in your freezer and periodically check to ensure it reads 0° or below. A refrigerator freezer (which is opened frequently, resulting in temperature changes) should be used only for short-term storage. To keep foods safe for a longer period of time, use a free-standing freezer.

- Select plastic bags and containers specifically designed for freezing because they are thicker and keep flavors in and moisture out.

- Use combination wrapping. For example, first wrap in freezer paper or plastic wrap, then in a resealable plastic freezer bag; squeeze out as much air as possible. If you're using a rigid plastic container, first line it with a freezer bag to make it airtight.

- Put cooked food in the freezer as soon as possible after preparing it. Food that is very hot should be cooled first, so it won't raise the temperature of the freezer.

- To cool food quickly and evenly, transfer it to a shallow pan or divide it among several small shallow containers. Or place the hot pan in the sink on a cooling rack with cool water running underneath it. Help hot liquids like soups and sauces cool by stirring them frequently.

- Divide food into small, serving-size portions. This will allow hot foods to cool quicker. The smaller packages will also thaw faster.

- When preparing dishes to keep in the freezer and bake later, save space by storing just the food, not the container. (This also allows you to continue having often-used baking dishes available.) To do this, line your baking dish with plastic wrap, add the food, cover with plastic wrap and freeze.
  Once it has frozen, remove the plastic-wrapped food and place it in a freezer bag before returning it to the freezer. When it's time to cook the dish, remove the plastic wrap and place the food in its original container for baking.

Organizing Your Freezer

- Clearly label and date each item you put in the freezer. Write the date on purchased frozen foods as well so you know when you bought them.

- Use a magnetic pad of paper to keep an inventory of what's inside your freezer, including the date it was added. Plan meals according to your freezer inventory and use older items first.

- Square plastic containers nicely tuck into corners and stack well.

- Flat packages store better in the freezer. Place individual servings of food (like uncooked hamburger patties, raw boneless skinless chicken breasts, baked cookies) on a waxed paper-lined baking sheet, making sure the items aren't touching one another. Freeze until firm. Wrap items in freezer paper or plastic wrap, then transfer to a plastic freezer bag. Flat items will also thaw more quickly. Stack flat packages so that the largest is on the bottom.

- Group similar items together. Use gallon-size freezer bags or inexpensive plastic containers to hold vegetables, meats, baked goods, etc.

- Don't overload your freezer. There should be space between items so that air can circulate freely and maintain a constant temperature.

Stocking Your **Pantry**

Keeping a well-stocked cupboard can cut down considerably on the time it takes to plan and prepare meals. We even offer some ingredient alternatives when you're in a pinch.

Basic Baking and Cooking Items

Baking powder
Baking soda
Biscuit/baking mix
Bread crumbs (plain and seasoned)
Cake mixes
Chocolate (chips, powder, syrup, squares)
Cookie mixes
Cooking wines (red and white)
Corn bread mix
Corn syrup (light and dark)
Cornmeal
Cornstarch
Extracts (almond, lemon, peppermint, vanilla)
Flaked coconut
Flour (all-purpose, bread, cake, whole wheat)
Frosting (a variety of canned)
Gelatin (flavored and unflavored)
Nonstick cooking spray
Nuts (chopped, ground, slivered, whole)
Oils (canola, olive, peanut, sesame, vegetable)
Pizza crust mix
Pudding (cook-and-serve and instant)
Quick bread/muffin mixes
Shortening
Sugar (brown, confectioners' and granulated)
Vinegars (balsamic, cider, white, red wine, rice wine, white wine)

Beverages

Coffee (instant and ground)
Fruit juice (a variety, including lemon and lime)
Milk (evaporated, powdered and sweetened condensed)
Tea (bags and instant)

Canned Fish/Seafood and Meats

Chicken   Salmon
Crabmeat   Tuna

Condiments and Sauces

Barbecue sauce
Hoisin sauce
Honey
Horseradish
Hot pepper sauce
Ice cream toppings
Jams, jellies and preserves
Ketchup
Maple syrup
Mayonnaise and/or salad dressing
Molasses
Mustards (coarse ground, Dijon and yellow)
Olives (green and ripe)
Pasta sauces (a variety)
Peanut butter
Pickles (sweet and dill)
Roasted sweet red peppers
Salad dressings
Salsa and picante sauces
Sloppy joe sauce
Soy sauce
Taco and chili seasoning mixes
Worcestershire sauce

Fruits and Vegetables

Beans (canned and dried black, cannellini, chickpeas, garbanzo, kidney)
Canned fruits (applesauce, apricots, cranberry sauce, mandarin oranges, peaches, pears, etc.)
Canned tomatoes (crushed, diced, paste, sauce, stewed, whole)
Canned vegetables (artichoke hearts, beans, carrots corn, hominy, peas, potatoes, pumpkin, etc.)
Dried fruits (apricots, cherries, cranberries, raisins)
Mushrooms (cans and jars)
Onions (fresh red and yellow)
Pie fillings (a variety)
Potatoes (a variety of fresh)

Grains

Barley (quick-cooking)
Cereal (oats and breakfast cereals)
Crackers (graham and assorted snack crackers)
Pasta (a variety of dried)
Rice (arborio, instant, long grain, wild rice mix)

Soups

Canned broth and bouillon granules (beef, chicken and vegetable)
Condensed soup (a variety)
Dry soup mixes (onion and vegetable)

Emergency Ingredient Substitutions

When You Need...	In This Amount...	Substitute...
Baking powder	1 teaspoon	1/2 teaspoon cream of tartar plus 1/4 teaspoon baking soda
Broth	1 cup	1 cup hot water plus 1 teaspoon bouillon granules *or* 1 bouillon cube
Buttermilk	1 cup	1 tablespoon lemon juice *or* vinegar plus enough milk to measure 1 cup; let stand 5 minutes. *Or* 1 cup plain yogurt
Cajun seasoning	1 teaspoon	1/2 to 1 teaspoon hot pepper sauce, 1/2 teaspoon dried thyme, 1/4 teaspoon dried basil and 1 minced garlic clove
Chocolate, semisweet	1 square (1 ounce)	1 square (1 ounce) unsweetened chocolate plus 1 tablespoon sugar *or* 3 tablespoons semisweet chocolate chips
Chocolate, unsweetened	1 square (1 ounce)	3 tablespoons baking cocoa plus 1 tablespoon shortening *or* vegetable oil
Cornstarch (for thickening)	1 tablespoon	2 tablespoons all-purpose flour
Corn syrup, dark	1 cup	3/4 cup light corn syrup plus 1/4 cup molasses
Corn syrup, light	1 cup	1 cup sugar plus 1/4 cup water
Cracker crumbs	1 cup	1 cup dry bread crumbs
Cream, half-and-half	1 cup	1 tablespoon melted butter plus enough whole milk to measure 1 cup
Egg	1 whole	2 egg whites *or* 2 egg yolks *or* 1/4 cup egg substitute
Garlic, fresh	1 clove	1/8 teaspoon garlic powder
Gingerroot, fresh	1 teaspoon	1/4 teaspoon ground ginger
Honey	1 cup	1-1/4 cups sugar plus 1/4 cup water
Lemon juice	1 teaspoon	1/4 teaspoon cider vinegar
Lemon peel	1 teaspoon	1/2 teaspoon lemon extract
Milk	1 cup	1/2 cup evaporated milk plus 1/2 cup water *or* 1 cup water plus 1/3 cup nonfat dry milk powder
Molasses	1 cup	1 cup honey
Onion	1 small (1/3 cup chopped)	1 teaspoon onion powder *or* 1 tablespoon dried minced onion
Poultry seasoning	1 teaspoon	3/4 teaspoon rubbed sage plus 1/4 teaspoon dried thyme
Sour cream	1 cup	1 cup plain yogurt
Sugar	1 cup	1 cup packed brown sugar *or* 2 cups sifted confectioners' sugar
Tomato juice	1 cup	1/2 cup tomato sauce plus 1/2 cup water
Tomato sauce	2 cups	3/4 cup tomato paste plus 1 cup water

General Recipe Index

This handy index lists every recipe by food category, major ingredient and/or cooking method, so you can easily locate recipes to suit your needs.

330